ABOUT THIS SERIES

Careers Without College is designed to help those who don't have a four-year college degree (and don't plan on getting one any time soon) find a career that fits their interests, talents, and personalities. It's for you if you're about to choose your career—or if you're planning to change careers and don't want to invest a lot of time or money in more education or training, at least not right at the start.

Some of the jobs featured do require an associate degree; others only require on-the-job training that may take a year, a few months, or only a few weeks. In today's real world, with its increasingly competitive job market, you may want to eventually consider getting a two- or maybe a four-year college degree in order to move up.

Careers Without College has up-to-date information that comes from extensive interviews with experts in each field. It's fresh, it's exciting, and it's easy to read. Plus, each book gives you something unique: an insider's look at the featured jobs through interviews with people who work in them now.

Peggy Schmidt

D1408668

Acknowledgements

Special thanks to the following people and organizations for their contributions to this book.

Alliance of American Insurers, Schaumberg, Illinois

Automotive Service Industry Association, Elk Grove Village, Illinois

Center for Professional Studies, Rochester Hills, Michigan

Doug Clemens, Huron Technical Training Center, Ford Motor Company, New Boston, Michigan

Rick Hersterberg, Public Relations, Toyota Motor Manufacturing Corporation, Georgetown, Kentucky

Stu Lasser, Owner, Saturn of Livingston, Livingston, New Jersey

Donna Louvre, Public Relations, Chubb Group, Florham Park, New Jersey

Janelle McCammon, Public Relations, General Motors Acceptance Corporation, Detroit, Michigan

Larry Miller, Owner, Miller Toyota, Salt Lake City, Utah

National Institute for Automotive Service Excellence and National Automotive Technicians Education Foundation, McLean, Virginia

Dave Roznowski, Public Relations, Johnson Controls, Inc., Plymouth, Michigan

Carl Sewell, Owner, Sewell Village Cadillac, Dallas, Texas

Chuck Snearly, Public Relations, Ford Motor Company, Dearborn, Michigan

Society of Automotive Engineers, Warrendale, Pennsylvania

Society of Manufacturing Engineers, Dearborn, Michigan

Karen Stewart, Public Relations, Lear Corporation, Southfield, Michigan

Carol Waldowski, Public Relations, General Motors Corporation, Warren, Michigan

Pam Whitaker, Claims Manager, Safeco, Stone Mountain, Georgia

Harold Wolchok, Professor, Bronx Community College, Bronx, New York

Ken Zino, Public Relations, Ford Motor Company, Dearborn, Michigan

CARES
WITHOUT
COLLEGE

CARS

COMPLETELY REVISED

Second Edition

Series developed by Peggy Schmidt

Peterson's
Thomson Learning™

Australia • Canada • Denmark • Japan • Mexico • New Zealand • Philippines
Puerto Rico • Singapore • South Africa • Spain • United Kingdom • United States

Visit Peterson's Education Center on the Internet (World Wide Web) at www.petersons.com

Copyright © 1999 Peggy Schmidt

Previous edition © 1992 by Peggy Schmidt

ISBN 0-7689-0265-7

Printed in Canada

10 9 8 7 6 5 4 3 2 1

Text Photo Credits
Pages: Chapter 1 opener, 18, 36, 56: © Martha Tabor/Working Images Photographs

What's in This Book

WHY THESE CAR CAREERS?

The automobile industry is a linchpin in the economy of the United States. Just about every household in the U.S. owns at least one car. Some have two or three. On any given day, 200 million cars and trucks travel the nation's roadways. About 30 million times a year, U.S. consumers buy or lease a new or used car, truck, or van. And perhaps most importantly, one in seven jobs in this country depends on the automotive industry.

This book features five careers in the auto industry. They include:

❑ CAD (computer-aided design) specialist
❑ Car salesperson
❑ Mechanic
❑ Claims representative
❑ Electronics specialist

Each was selected because it is a career that does not require a four-year college degree. In fact, while some require specialized training, only one requires a two-year associate degree. Job openings are predicted to be plentiful in these careers throughout this decade and beyond. The work of people in each of these careers is important to the future of the car business.

A CAD specialist is in on the earliest stages of the birth of an automobile. Using the most modern computer technology available, the CAD specialist works with engineers and designers to create the blueprint for the car and its parts. Demand for CAD specialists far exceeds the supply, the pay is good, and the potential for advancement is excellent. Because the technology is new and ever changing, a CAD specialist faces exciting challenges.

Once a car is manufactured, someone must demonstrate and sell it. The role of the car salesperson in the dealership is a changing one. The basic job remains the same; but with the increased emphasis on customer satisfaction, the salesperson has become the dealership's goodwill ambassador as well. Increased attention is also being placed on the job satisfaction of the salesperson. Dealerships are experimenting with ways to reward and keep good sales personnel beyond the reward that's always been there—making a good salary from commissions.

No matter how well a car is manufactured, it's going to need servicing and repair over its lifetime. Today's mechanic must use a computer as well as nuts and bolts because electronics are increasingly controlling car systems. It's still a job that requires getting your hands dirty, but it's one that pays a good hourly rate and is recession proof.

With more cars on the road than ever, the chance of accidents increases; so do jobs for auto claims representatives. They are the people who decide how much money car owners who have been in accidents are entitled to receive. Jobs are available in just about every small town and major city across the country. And insurance companies offer claims reps good potential for advancement.

There are more electronics in today's automobiles than on the first lunar module that landed on the moon, and the factories that produce today's modern motor vehicles are filled with electronics as well. Robots weld and paint the cars, apply waterproof sealant around the doors, and install the windshields. Programmable controllers take measurements to insure the vehicle's frame is put together properly. Driverless guided vehicles carry the parts to the assembly line. All of these devices contain sophisticated electronics that must constantly be maintained and programmed to keep the assembly line moving smoothly. Unlike the assembly line worker of the past who may have twisted the same kind of bolt hundreds of times a day, the electronics specialist faces new challenges every day—and is rewarded accordingly.

If you are someone who is into cars, there is a good chance you will be able to find a place in the automotive industry that is right for you.

Jac Nasser

On Cars and Your Future

Jac Nasser is the President and Chief Operating Officer of Ford Motor Company, the second largest corporation in the world. Yet Nasser, born in a remote village in Lebanon and raised in Australia, started out as just a young man who loved cars. Like many teenage boys, he could spot the make and model of a car half a mile away. He wanted a career where he could build and drive cars.

As a teenager, he enjoyed working on cars and considered a technical career. But he notes, "You had to take drafting, and I couldn't draw a straight line." So Nasser went into business management at Ford.

Nasser was rapidly promoted all the way to the top of Ford Motor Company because of his remarkable ability to quickly understand and solve difficult problems. He has served Ford on five continents in a wide array of assignments. He speaks several languages, but his favorite language is "car talk." Nasser enjoys talking about cars and trucks with designers, engineers, factory workers, dealership service technicians, and anyone else who shares his passion for automobiles and the global automotive business.

Today, Jac Nasser is positioning Ford to become the world's leading consumer company that provides automotive products and services. To achieve that vision, he is expanding Ford's business beyond automotive manufacturing and into related industries such as automotive repair and recycling.

We asked Jac Nasser to advise our readers about careers without college in the automotive industry.

When Henry Ford established the assembly line and put the world on wheels, he was proud of the fact that any factory employee could learn his or her job in just a few minutes. Today, it takes much longer than that to start a career in the automotive industry, but it's a lot more rewarding.

The automotive industry has changed dramatically in the past 25 years. Cars were once designed on paper by draftsmen, tested on a track, and built by hand in factories. Today, technicians work with computer-aided design, computer-simulated testing, and computer-aided manufacturing.

At the dealership, self-taught mechanics have been replaced by highly trained and certified service technicians. They use computers to diagnose problems and video-conferencing to consult with company engineers.

Even with all of this advanced technology, there are still jobs in the auto industry for people without college degrees.

Many outstanding career opportunities exist in manufacturing and in the dealership service technician ranks. But the nature of the jobs and the qualities of the people that companies seek have changed.

First, every auto worker, no matter what his or her job, is expected to continue to learn. Ford Motor Company, for example, is now as much like a campus as a manufacturing company. Every employee, from senior executives to new factory workers, is expected to take classes to keep pace with the changing world. That's because knowledge, particularly technical knowledge, is growing at incredible rates.

Much of what anyone learns in school will be obsolete in a few years. So the technical employees we hire today must be enthusiastic about learning, as continuous education will be a significant part of their careers.

Second, we need individuals with problem-solving skills. Computer technology has freed individuals from repetitive tasks. That allows them to do what only human beings can do—think, create, and innovate.

Third, we need people who can work effectively in teams. Virtually every employee in Ford Motor Company is a member of one or more teams.

The automobile is incredibly complicated. No one individual can know it all or hope to keep up with all of its rapidly changing technology. And no one area of expertise can be effective unless it's thoroughly integrated with other areas. So we work in teams to pool our knowledge and problem-solving skills.

Finally, we need individuals who are willing and able to communicate. At Ford, we say that the opportunity to learn comes with the responsibility to teach and to share information and ideas with team members.

The auto industry is an exciting business. It's changing rapidly as automobiles, the factories that produce them, and the service centers that repair them make the transition into the computer age. The auto industry is now one of the greatest consumers and producers of new technology in the world.

But there are still important, rewarding, and lucrative jobs in the auto industry for individuals without college degrees. That's especially true for people who get training beyond high school in technical schools and those who earn associate degrees at community colleges. And it's even more true for those who are interested in continuing to learn and to apply that learning throughout their careers.

FAMOUS BEGINNINGS

Lee Iacocca, Retired Chairman of Chrysler Corporation

No one is better known in the automotive industry than Lee Iacocca. He began his career selling cars in Pennsylvania and then joined the Ford Motor Company, where he developed the Mustang and eventually climbed through the ranks to president. Iacocca later moved to Chrysler Corporation, saving it from bankruptcy. He retired from Chrysler in 1992 and is now involved with EV Global Motors Company, a California firm that sells battery-powered bicycles.

Roger S. Penske, Race Car Owner, Car Dealer, Repair Shop Owner, Industrialist

Roger Penske is the founder and president of Penske Corporation. He started out as a sales engineer with ALCOA and as a part-time racecar driver. Today, he co-owns and operates ten professional motorsports facilities throughout the U.S., and his Penske Racing is among the most successful car racing teams in history. He owns Detroit Diesel Corporation, a major manufacturer of diesel engines, as well as automotive retail operations that include dealerships, Penske Auto Centers, and the Penske Truck Leasing Company.

Mike Jackson, President and Chief Executive Officer, Mercedes-Benz of North America, Inc.

Mike Jackson started his automotive career as a mechanic in a Mercedes-Benz dealership. He worked his way up to management and eventually bought his own Mercedes-Benz dealership. In the late 1980s, when Mercedes-Benz sales were in the doldrums, Jackson was elected by fellow dealers to serve as their spokesman. Jackson became such an outspoken critic of the automaker that Mercedes gave him a job in 1990 to head sales and marketing. He was named president and chief executive officer in 1998.

CAD SPECIALIST

Do you like cars, computers, and the excitement of being on the cutting edge of technology? If so, the high demand for people trained in computer-aided design (CAD) could put you in the driver's seat.

A CAD specialist (also called a CAD technician) uses a computer to prepare technical drawings and plans for a car or the various parts of a car. It's only been in the last twenty years that the computer has nearly replaced paper, pencil, and the drawing board in the auto design business.

How does the process work? First, engineers decide what they generally want to have in the car part—for example, a camshaft. They pass this information to the CAD designer, who creates a layout of the camshaft on a computer screen. The layout then goes to the CAD detailer who produces a highly specific diagram containing the exact measurements and information needed to build the camshaft. CAD detailers can create a three-dimensional model on the computer screen.

At this point, the CAD diagram of the camshaft goes back to the engineers. They explore whether anything should be done differently, run some tests, and make any changes they feel are needed. The CAD specialist then revises the diagram. When everyone agrees that the part design is what they want, the CAD diagram goes to the machinists, manufacturers, and suppliers who will make the camshaft. (In the most technically advanced compa-

1

nies, this information is transferred to the parts makers by computer instead of on a paper blueprint.)

Then a specialist in computer-aided manufacturing (CAM) uses computer systems to actually build the part. The CAM specialist programs, monitors, and often repairs the machine or network of machines, including robots, that produce the part.

CAD is more accurate and a lot faster than manually drawing a part, and it creates a permanent record that can be accessed at any time to verify part specifications. Before CAD, designers would draw a part blueprint that would become the master. The model makers would make a model from it; the tool makers would use it to make tools and fixtures to produce the part. But there would be little mistakes built in all along the way—the slightest mistake would compound itself.

Computer-aided drafting also speeds up the process of getting a product to market. Today, automobile and parts manufacturers are heavily recruiting potential CAD employees through placement offices at community colleges and vocational training centers. Many companies offer internships and co-op programs to students who are working on their associate's degree.

What You Need to Know

- ❏ Computer basics
- ❏ Factory machine operations that produce parts
- ❏ Properties of metals and plastics used in machine parts
- ❏ Basic engineering principles
- ❏ Mathematics (algebra, geometry, trigonometry)
- ❏ Science (chemistry and physics)

Necessary Skills

- ❏ Ability to read blueprints
- ❏ Drafting skills

Do You Have What It Takes?

- ❏ Problem-solving mindset; ability to identify a problem, organize evidence, and deduce a probable solution
- ❏ Determination to stay with a problem or project until it is successfully completed
- ❏ Ability to accept criticism without taking it personally
- ❏ Flexibility to make design changes over and over
- ❏ Neatness, accuracy, and attention to detail
- ❏ Willingness to spend many hours in front of a computer
- ❏ Ability to communicate well with others—ask questions, take direction, and apply it to the situation

Education

An associate degree in auto body design, CAD, or what is often called applied sciences is required; increasingly, four-year college degrees are preferred. Course work or experience in drafting is helpful. Community college or technical school courses should include descriptive geometry, basic engineering (including hydraulics, pneumatics, and

Getting into the Field

electronics), data processing, and computer training in computer-aided design software programs.

Licenses Required

None

Job Outlook

Job openings will grow: at an average rate. Opportunities will be most plentiful for those with at least two years of drafting training and experience using CAD systems.

The Ground Floor

Entry-level job: detailer
Everyone starts off as a detailer, which provides the on-the-job training needed to move to designer. Some people continue to work as detailers throughout their careers. Others can move up to designer within a few years.

On-the-Job Responsibilities

Beginners (CAD detailers)

❑ Meet with designers and engineers on what the car or car part will include
❑ Produce three-dimensional diagram of the car part design from the designer's layout on the computer
❑ Make changes to the diagram required by the designers and engineers

Experienced Designers

❑ Work with engineers to decide what a car or car part will include
❑ Produce a computer layout or drawing of how the part will generally look
❑ Supervise the work of the detailer
❑ Explore options for the design or other materials that could be used
❑ Seek approval from engineers on completed design

When You'll Work

CAD specialists work a standard 40-hour week. Overtime is often necessary when the deadline for a project is approaching.

Large companies employing CAD specialists offer two to three weeks of paid vacation and all major holidays off.

❑ Pension plans
❑ Stock purchase plans are offered by General Motors Corporation, Ford Motor Company, and DaimlerChrysler AG and some large, publicly held auto parts companies. (In such plans, for every share purchased by the employee, the company buys a share or part of a share for that employee.)
❑ Courses offered at the workplace to keep CAD designers on top of the latest technological developments
❑ Tuition reimbursement for college courses in design, engineering, technology, or business management to become more highly skilled or to advance on the job

❑ All auto manufacturers
❑ Major auto parts manufacturers

Beginners and experienced workers: little or no travel potential

CAD specialists work in clean, comfortable, and quiet offices. They spend most of their day alone or with one other person at a computer workstation.

❑ Susceptibility to eyestrain
❑ Potential for back discomfort (from long periods of sitting)
❑ Hand and wrist problems (from long periods at the computer)

Dollars and Cents

Because demand for CAD specialists is high, the pay is good. The starting salary for an entry-level CAD detailer is $10 to $16 per hour. Many specialists double that rate within 5 years. Part-time trainers earn $40 to $55 an hour. Some top CAD specialists make as much as $100 per hour.

Moving Up

CAD specialists advance quickly because of the shortage of skilled workers in this field. Continued education is required to keep up with the fast-changing technology, and companies offer on-the-job training. Many CAD specialists obtain their four-year college degrees in design, engineering, or technology while they work so they can become engineers who design and engineer cars and car parts or advance into supervisory positions.

Where the Jobs Are

Jobs are concentrated in the Midwest, particularly Michigan and Ohio, where most automobile and automobile parts manufacturing takes place.

School Information

Most high schools and vocational high schools offer drafting courses; some also offer CAD classes. Some for-profit vocational schools, particularly those in the Midwest, offer courses and certificates in CAD.

Community colleges offer CAD courses leading to a two-year associate degree in auto body design. In particular, community colleges in Midwestern manufacturing centers have co-op programs (which alternate classroom learning with on-the-job training) with local auto and auto parts companies.

The Male/Female Equation

Traditional drafting and design have been dominated by men, but women are increasingly entering the computer-aided design field. The auto companies are aggressively recruiting women and minorities for positions.

The Bad News

❑ Economic downturns can result in layoffs
❑ Eyestrain from intense computer work
❑ Deadline pressure can be stressful
❑ Jobs confined to a limited geographic area

The Good News

❑ Good pay and benefits
❑ Excellent potential for advancement with additional training and education
❑ Opportunity to work with state-of-the-art technology
❑ Design skills can be transferred to other industries, from architecture to aerospace

The Society of Automotive Engineers offers a free brochure, "Automotive Engineering: A Moving Career." Write to:

Society of Automotive Engineers
400 Commonwealth Drive
Warrendale, Pennsylvania 15096
724-776-4841

Additional information can be attained by contacting:

American Design Drafting Association
P.O. Box 11937
Columbia, South Carolina 29211
803-771-0008
World Wide Web: http://www.adda.org

Accrediting Commission of Career Schools
 and Colleges of Technology
2101 Wilson Boulevard, Suite 302
Arlington, Virginia 22201
703-247-4212
World Wide Web: http://www.accsct.org

Making Your Decision: What to Consider

More Information Please

Center for Professional Studies
811 South Boulevard, Suite 200
Rochester Hills, Michigan 48307
248-844-9090
E-mail: info@profstudies.com
World Wide Web: http://www.profstudies.com

WHAT IT'S REALLY LIKE

Wendy McCurdy, 27
Contract CAD Specialist to General Motors
Global Technology Associates
Warren, Michigan
Years in the business: two

What got you into the automotive industry?
I was always fascinated with cars. My twin sister and my father are in the field; she's a designer and my dad is a senior designer. Their influence and my own curiosity were both factors.

What is your educational background?
I went to Macomb Community College. I took general courses because I didn't know what I wanted to do. My sister suggested I take a drafting course, and I liked it, so I took more. I earned an associate degree in general studies–applied science of vehicle design and a vehicle design certificate.

Do you know a lot about cars?
No. One of the biggest misconceptions about the CAD field is that you need to know a lot about them, but that isn't the case. I also thought you needed tons of math and science, which I'm not good at. But you don't need it. Drafting skills are what's most important.

How did you land your first job?
I started in a co-op program with Global Technology Associates, a contractor to General Motors.

What did you do?

I was in the electrical department designing wiring harness systems. General Motors' CAD system is fairly new, so I spent the first 10 weeks in classroom training. Then I practiced. I was assigned the job of converting parts from the old CAD system into the new system where the information is stored in the database.

Would you recommend a co-op program for young people who want to go into CAD?

Yes. It's very structured. You can see how to move from Point A to Point B in your profession. You alternate between six months of work and six months of schooling, then you go back to work for six months before you graduate. You also have a good chance of getting hired when you graduate.

What are you working on now?

I'm modeling a section of a new small car and transferring the information from the old system to the new. The section is constantly being changed, which involves meetings with engineers and designers.

Who do you work with?

I interact with engineers most of the time. I have a design leader and a supervisor as well as other people doing the details of the design work on the CAD system. So you need good social and communication skills.

How much time do you spend at the computer?

A big misconception is that you are alone in front of a computer screen all the time. Some days I'm there all day; other days I'm moving around. In the co-op program, we took field trips to various facilities, like the testing grounds for vehicles, the wind tunnel, and the styling studio.

What advice would you give a young person considering the CAD field?

I definitely would suggest a two-year training program.

What kind of personality traits does a CAD job require?

You have to be enthusiastic, patient, and friendly. It helps to be social and outgoing. You have to be willing to accept challenges.

What is the best part of your job?

The continuous education. You are constantly offered classes. I just finished an advanced modeling class, for which I received certification. Now I'm looking at other classes for certification. You are always challenged with new ideas and new technology. It's interesting because you are not doing the same thing all the time. You also have the ability to move around. I can work on the exterior parts of the car or the chassis or the underbody.

Do you feel you have opportunities to advance in the field?

Most definitely. I have an opportunity of a lifetime here.

Is the field as open to women as men?

Yes. Sometimes I feel I have an advantage being a woman. And more women are moving into the field. When I first started school, my classes of 30 people averaged one or two women. When I go back for classes now, there are five or six.

What do you hope to do in the future?

I want to work directly for General Motors. My mentor in the co-op program is a female chassis engineer. I'm considering engineering or being an engineering technician. That requires a bachelor's degree in vehicle design. There are a few colleges that now offer such a degree.

Laura Vargo, 36
Studio engineer
Lear Corporation
Southfield, Michigan
Years in the business: 15

What was your first job in the automotive industry?

I worked in a small graphics design department of what was then the Chrysler Corporation. I created graphics for presentations and brochures on the computer. It was my first exposure to computer graphics, and I realized that was the direction I wanted to pursue.

How did you get the job?

I was in a graphics design program at Macomb Community College. One of my instructors recommended me for a summer job. That turned into a full-time job. I was there for two years.

Did you pursue more schooling in graphics design?

I continued with basic courses at the community college, but it did not offer computer graphics.

What did you do after you left Chrysler?

I took a job with Electronic Data Systems at General Motors' Design Center. I didn't work on the computers, but I supported the designers who were using the system.

How were computers used in the design studio?

The designers would generate a two-dimensional design of a car, and this new tool would create three-dimensional models.

How did you learn to use the technology?

I'm basically self-taught. I became proficient at the system and began to teach it to the rest of the designers, sculptors, and engineers at the Design Center. I was in that role for some time.

What was your next job?

I joined Lear Corporation, a supplier of interior systems, including seats. I work as a studio engineer. Now I'm the person who generates the three-dimensional models.

What is a typical day like?

I communicate with the designer and the engineer. I work on the computer developing a seat. We build the seat on the computer to the designer's specifications and the engineer's criteria. They use information from my CAD model to build a prototype for testing. We then go back in to make changes.

What do you like most about your job?

It is very challenging. I also like the combination of the technical and creative. There's also a lot of opportunity for growth.

What do you like least about your job?

In addition to doing my job, I have to keep up with technology that is changing really fast. I don't ever want to become unmarketable, so I have to push myself to get my job done and keep my skills up to date. I network to learn new things and new ways of using the technology.

What education or training does a person need to get into the field?

A number of community colleges and universities offer programs in CAD. Small companies offer specialized computer training on their particular equipment or software programs.

What kind of person is likely to be most successful in this field?

You need to be able to communicate with different types of people. Designers are quite different from engineers. Designers sketch the general ideas for a vehicle, while the engineers focus on the details of how it goes together.

13

Do you need to know about cars or be mechanically inclined?
You have to learn certain technical skills, but you don't have to know about cars per se. I didn't know anything about cars when I started. I learned on the job.

What is your proudest professional achievement?
I traveled to Australia, Germany, and Brazil to train more than 200 General Motors design employees on the technology.

Dennis Cherry, 44
Lead Design Engineer
Johnson Controls, Inc.
Plymouth, Michigan
Years in the business: 27

How did you get into CAD work?
I had been attending college, where I was majoring in medical technology. I had taken four years of shop and drafting in high school, so I worked summer jobs in drafting to pay the bills. I realized I could make a good living drafting and went to work for an electronic communication company in drafting and design.

Did you get a college degree?
I got an associate degree in math, technology, and natural sciences from Washtenaw Community College in Ann Arbor, Michigan.

How did you make the move from drafting to CAD?
I had moved to Ann Arbor, Michigan, to work at an engineering company. I did electronic drafting, which is using machines to do the drawings instead of working on a board with paper and pencil. At the same time, I was also taking classes at the community college, and a recruiter from Hoover Universal, an auto parts company later purchased by Johnson Controls, Inc., interviewed and hired

me as an automotive drafter. The company, which designs, engineers, and manufactures complete car interiors from door trim to seats, got a CAD system in 1981. I could see it was the wave of the future. CAD has three-dimensional capability. I saw it as a tool that had the capability of creating on the screen what I was seeing in my head.

What training did you receive?

I went to Chicago for training at a computer company.

What has been your career path in CAD?

I started as a detail draftsman, on the old-fashioned drafting career path. My job was to take the layout drawings for a part for a car from the layout engineers and create detailed drawings on the drafting board. Then I moved to lead designer, and then to a CAD specialist. A couple of years ago, I went on to be design supervisor. I do some engineering, analyze CAD methods, and work on applications for CAD.

How has CAD changed the way things work at your company?

When I started at Hoover Universal in the early 1980s, we were a five-person department. Today, there are hundreds of CAD engineers and even more people, like the engineers and purchasing people, who use the CAD data. The goal is for all people who make decisions on a project to view the CAD designs and understand them; not too many people can read drawings. With CAD, they can see a part and see it move. As they say, a picture is worth a thousand words.

Has the career path changed since you were in drafting?

CAD has blended everything together. And there's a big difference between a CAD operator and CAD designer. CAD designers have to design something, have it tested, and see it built. Over time they develop a sense of what works and what doesn't. A CAD operator learns how to run the system, like learning how to use a laptop, but doesn't design things.

Why is CAD such a growing field?

The automakers are shortening the lead times to develop new vehicles and cutting costs. CAD helps that happen. DaimlerChrysler, Ford, and General Motors are moving to digital mock-up assembly where they create three-dimensional shaded models to build assemblies and prototypes on the computer, not by hand. They then do the testing and development on computer, too. The eventual goal is to become paperless. Another advantage is that I can have all the technology in place in my laptop, and it can be distributed to people around the globe. People can work on a part or vehicle by day in England and others at night in Australia.

How are CAD and other computer technologies changing?

CAD is changing rapidly. DaimlerChrysler, for instance, is doing a complete crash test of a vehicle on computer. The big wave now in CAD is an emphasis on procedures and methodology. Companies are coming up with best practices guidelines for all those using CAD throughout their corporations.

With the technology changing so rapidly, how do you get your training?

I took time out of my work day to learn more on my own. I also took formal classes from vendors of the technology. A lot of what we do is on the edge of technology and is customized for our customers' needs.

What do you like most about your job?

I'm a problem solver. I like the challenge of figuring something out. That's why I switched from doing design to more applications work. I like to try to figure out how something works and make it work well.

What do you like least about your job?

There's not enough time in the day to do everything.

What is your proudest achievement?

I worked on a team for a new seat frame. We took a concept and developed it with the engineer to create an all-new product that was a lightweight, tubular seat frame for the Dodge Neon. We received a patent for the design.

What kind of person is most likely to succeed in CAD?

A CAD specialist should be someone who as the initiative to take a concept and develop it. The person should know when to ask questions and be assertive in pushing an issue. Then he or she has to take the information, think about it, and put it into the product. You should be a problem solver and an abstract thinker. You need to be persistent in finding information and ultimately the answer.

SALESPERSON

The days of the stereotypical fast-talking car salesman in the gaudy plaid jacket are gone. Today's car salesperson is a professional who not only sells the car but is also an ambassador for the dealership. If you're a fan of automobile shows, find yourself talking about the latest models on the market, and love to test drive anyone's new car, a job in automobile sales may be for you.

Previous sales experience is a big plus; salespeople from other businesses often move into car sales because they can make more money through bigger commissions. If you have no previous sales experience, a common first job in automobile sales is on a dealership's used car lot.

Since the salesperson is the first contact the customer has with the dealership, he or she has the best shot at making a good impression. Customer satisfaction is the name of the game in the automobile business today, so you need to pay attention to what customers are saying and what they are asking for.

To be successful, it helps to be outgoing and persuasive. You must be willing to work long hours and make cold telephone calls to people you don't know who might turn out to be prospective customers. You must be good at

19

building relationships with customers so they'll come back to buy their next vehicle from you or refer people they know to you. If you're good, you can make big bucks...and you can drive home a different model every night if you want to.

What You Need to Know

- ❑ What the various parts of a car (or van, truck, or other vehicle) are called and how they work
- ❑ A general understanding of how the automotive industry works and your specific competition
- ❑ History of the cars/models you're selling
- ❑ Car finance options so you can make recommendations to customers

Necessary Skills

- ❑ Sales experience helpful
- ❑ Basic math skills (to figure out monthly payments on a car at various interest rates and loan periods)
- ❑ Familiarity with a calculator
- ❑ Good driving skills
- ❑ Familiarity with computers (new car ordering systems are on computers)

Do You Have What It Takes?

- ❑ A friendly, outgoing personality
- ❑ A well-groomed appearance
- ❑ The power of persuasion
- ❑ Ability to maintain your cool when customers become difficult or rude
- ❑ A positive attitude that allows you to shrug off rejection
- ❑ Patience—you'll often be on your feet most of the day
- ❑ A good telephone manner
- ❑ Discipline to organize your workday
- ❑ Motivation to initiate sales calls
- ❑ Ability to negotiate and make compromises so that you can close a deal

Education

A high school diploma is required. Additional education may give you an edge over other job candidates. Courses in sales and business management are helpful.

Job Outlook

The Ground Floor

**On-the-Job
Responsibilities**

Licenses Required

Driver's license. Clean driving record.

Although the number of car dealerships will continue to decrease because bigger dealers are buying up smaller dealers and merging the operations, openings in car and truck sales will remain numerous because of the high employee turnover rate. Jobs are very competitive at dealerships that carry top-priced cars and the models in highest demand.

Entry-level job: salesperson
Large dealerships have a number of entry-level positions that can help prepare you for a job in new vehicle sales. They include:

- ❑ Used car salesperson
- ❑ Service adviser (writes up repair orders and sells the services a dealership provides)
- ❑ Parts and accessories salesperson

Beginners

- ❑ Meet prospective customers at the door or on the car lot
- ❑ Explain the technical aspects and safety features of the car and its advantages over the competition
- ❑ Discuss optional features available on the car
- ❑ Go over warranties, financing arrangements, and insurance programs sold by the dealership
- ❑ Take customers on demonstration rides and drives
- ❑ Negotiate the final sale
- ❑ Maintain a list of prospects and regularly contact customers
- ❑ Meet sales goals (set by the sales manager on a weekly, monthly, or quarterly basis)

Experienced Employees (sales managers)

Do all of the above, plus

- ❏ Manage and motivate the sales force
- ❏ Provide training to sales staff
- ❏ Assist with negotiations
- ❏ Approve the final deals
- ❏ Hire and fire salespeople

Experienced Employees (fleet managers)

- ❏ Deal with business customers who buy several vehicles at a time

When You'll Work

Get ready for long hours—often 60 to 80 hours a week. Salespeople usually work Monday through Friday and one day of the weekend, including some evenings. Some dealerships give salespeople a day off during the week.

The busiest times of the year are the fall, when new vehicles are introduced by the manufacturers, and spring, when the winter doldrums are over and better weather lures customers into the showroom. But whether customer traffic is slow or busy, the showroom must be staffed constantly.

Time Off

Vacations are usually scheduled for the winter months, when sales are traditionally low. Beyond that, only major holidays—Thanksgiving, Christmas, and Easter—are paid days off.

Perks

- ❏ Manufacturer discounts (about five percent) on vehicles sold by the dealership
- ❏ Overnight use of new dealership vehicles

Who's Hiring

- ❏ Dealerships employ about 1 million people. In 1998, there were 22,367 new car dealerships in the U.S.
- ❏ Used car dealers

Places You'll Go

Beginners and experienced salespeople: little travel potential

The exception is a trip for an occasional training seminar offered in locations that can be reached by car.

Surroundings

The car salesperson works in a clean, well-lit environment with large windows looking out on the dealership property, which is usually located on a busy avenue or in a central business district. He or she is likely to have a desk or a small office off the main showroom. The salesperson must also go outdoors frequently to show vehicles that are parked there.

Dollars and Cents

The average car salesperson earns $19,900 a year. However, a well-established salesperson who attracts many return customers can earn as much as $100,000 a year. Most salespeople are paid on commission, that is, a percentage or a flat fee for each vehicle they sell. A percentage commission is usually about 25 percent of the dealer's gross profit on the sale, so the better the deal the salesperson negotiates, the bigger his or her profit. A large luxury car has a higher profit margin than a small, low-priced car. A very popular model has a higher profit margin than does a slow seller.

The flat fees that some dealerships pay usually range from $50 to $75 for each car or truck sold. Some dealerships provide a minimal base salary in addition to commissions. Others pay a base salary if the commissions for the week are lower than the salary. Some provide minimal base salary to new salespeople and gradually decrease and eliminate the salary once the salesperson is established and is regularly earning commissions.

Moving Up

The more vehicles you sell, the better your chances of moving into a manager's spot, supervising the work of other salespeople. In addition to being a super salesperson, you must also be able to work well with all kinds of people, know how to delegate work, and have the skills and enthusiasm to motivate others.

Earning your certificate from the National Automobile Dealers Association, the industry trade group for new car dealerships, is useful for advancement or for making a move to another dealership. Taking classes on your own in business management, accounting, or sales training can also help you improve your skills and shows your bosses that you're serious about getting ahead.

The next step above sales manager is general manager, the person who overseas all of the operations of the dealership. Some dealers reward good managers by making them part owners in a dealership or helping them get established in their own dealership. Most dealers begin their careers in sales.

Dealerships are located in almost every city and town across the U.S., so sales jobs are widely available. More dealerships are located in large cities, and, not surprisingly, they often employ more people and handle a bigger volume of sales than those in outlying areas.

Where the Jobs Are

All automobile manufacturers provide training to salespeople at their dealerships. That training can involve anything from watching a videotape at the dealership to a weeklong seminar at an out-of-town location to learn all about the manufacturer's new product line.

Training

The National Automobile Dealers Association's training and certification program for salespeople consists of 12 hours of self-study and 8 hours of classroom instruction on ethical and legal practices, selling techniques, consumer psychology, customer loyalty, and sales manager training.

Men far outnumber women in automobile sales, but women are increasingly entering the field. They often have an advantage in selling to other women, who buy half the cars sold today.

The Male/Female Equation

Making Your Decision: What to Consider

The Bad News

- ❏ Usually no base salary or pension
- ❏ Long hours
- ❏ Earnings tied to ups and downs in the economy
- ❏ Stiff competition for customers
- ❏ Stereotype of being smooth talking and deceptive

The Good News

- ❏ Potential for high earnings
- ❏ Earnings relate to sales ability
- ❏ Good chance of advancing to management position
- ❏ Potential to own your own dealership
- ❏ Personal car discounts

More Information Please

Write for the free brochure, "Automotive Careers," which describes various careers in the retail end of the automobile industry.

National Automobile Dealers Association
8400 Westpark Drive
McLean, Virginia 22102
703-827-7407

WHAT IT'S REALLY LIKE

Pamela Hoffman, 36
Sales Consultant
Saturn of Livingston
Livingston, New Jersey
Years in the business: less than one year

How did you get in the car business?
I was driving home from my job as a waitress one day, wiped out. I saw the Saturn dealership where I had bought my car a few months earlier. I pulled into the parking lot and got an application. I was called in for an interview.

How did it go?
It was intimidating. Four men interviewed me. They threw questions at me because I had never sold cars. After a second interview, I was immediately hired.

How did your early days on the job go?
I was scared out of my mind. You receive a small salary during training, but then it is all commission when you start selling cars. Learning the other brands of cars on the used-car lot required doing research on my own. For the first month, I did a lot of reading and watched videos on the Saturn process. I trailed people and watched what they did.

What do you do on your job?
Saturn's main concern is which car is right for the customer. So I talk to a customer for five minutes before I show a car. They sit with me in my office and we discuss

what they want and need in a car. Then I tell them what's available to fit those needs and wants.

What do you emphasize when you're explaining the features of the car?

We focus a lot on the safety of the car, because Saturn is the safest car in its class. We have a cutaway of the car in the dealership, and I explain the safety features and why the insurance rates are lower. That's a big plus in New Jersey where insurance premiums are high.

What are your hours?

I get Sunday off and one day during the week. Saturdays are mandatory. I work three nights until 9 p.m.; I come in at 1 or 2 p.m. except for one day when I work from 9 a.m. to 9 p.m. I don't find the hours shocking, because I've worked in retail and the restaurant business. But the average person may not like them.

What's a typical day like?

I review the previous day and look at the list of people I spoke with the day before. If I didn't sell them a car, I send them a thank you note. Or, I may call a customer who shopped for a car to see how he or she is doing. Instead of grabbing customers as they come in the door, salespeople at Saturn dealerships have a rotation plan where they take turns being paged to meet a guest. There's a lot of down time when we're not busy. That's a good time to do more research.

What kind of personality traits does a salesperson need?

You have to believe in the product. You have to like and know the product. I probably wouldn't sell any other kind of car. You have to be a very patient and adaptable person. I had one customer who other salespeople would have put through a wall. But you can't take things personally, and you have to go with the flow.

Do you need to know a lot about cars to be a salesperson?

You don't have to be a mechanic; you need to be more of a people person. But a general knowledge of cars is helpful. I grew up in a family with boys—three older brothers. My dad was a tinkerer and was always fixing our car. I don't think he ever took it to a mechanic, so I was exposed to that at a young age. I still fix the small stuff on my own car. That experience was a plus in getting hired. If you have no desire to learn after you get the job, you are probably not right for the job either.

What is your educational background?

I studied fine arts in college, but I didn't finish.

What kind of education would you recommend to someone who wanted to become a salesperson?

I'd advise taking some college courses. You deal with people on many levels. The dealership I work for has an upper–middle-class clientele that is well educated. You need to sound educated and articulate.

How are you doing so far?

I'm averaging a car a day. The top salesperson sells about 24 cars a month; most average 12 to 18.

How do you like the job?

I'm loving this job. I look forward to going to work every morning. I didn't feel that way in my previous jobs. The people and atmosphere are pleasant. It doesn't feel cutthroat. In fact, I feel like my co-workers are cheering me on every step of the way.

What do you think your future prospects are in this business?

I feel once I learn more about the business, I'll have complete control over my destiny. In my previous job as a customer service representative, I didn't have that. It was up to someone else to promote me. I feel I can promote myself. It's up to me to make it happen.

Tom Batson, 31
Salesperson
Sewell Lexus
Dallas, Texas
Years in the business: nine

What was your first job in the automobile business?
When I was 16, I was a porter at a dealership in Odessa, Texas. I cleaned the cars and ran errands. It was great because I got to drive new cars all the time.

Have you always liked cars?
Yes. My friends and I started driving at early ages. We'd sneak out and drive our parents' cars when we were ten or eleven years old.

Are you mechanically inclined?
I used to tinker with cars, and still do tinker with anything mechanical, including boats or motorcycles.

What is your educational background?
I was in college, but didn't finish. I'm the last of the people in our store to not have a college degree. Now, the Sewell organization is requiring degrees.

How did you move up in the car business?
My first job after leaving college was as a salesperson in a parts department of a Toyota dealership. Within six months, I was the number one salesperson at the dealership. But I didn't like the dealership. The employees felt being mediocre was okay, which frustrated me.

So what did you do?
It was 1989, and I knew Toyota was coming out with a new luxury car and a new franchise called Lexus. I called Lexus to see who the dealer in Dallas was going to be. I was told it was to be Carl Sewell, the dealer I currently work for. I wanted to work in the parts department, but I was hired as a service adviser. I eventually became the service manager. In the early days, we spent our time prepping new cars that had been sold, because there were no cars on the road that needed service or maintenance.

Then, as more cars were sold and they got some miles on them, we started seeing them for service.

Why did you move to new car sales?

That's the natural progression in this company. If you are going to move up, you have to go through the new car sales department. Also, I had been in the service department for eight years. I'm still young and feel I haven't done everything I could do for myself. I wanted to take a chance to see if I could do something else.

Do you work exclusively on commission?

I now work on a 100 percent commission basis. The first month they offered me a guaranteed amount, but I earned that—plus some—and have been on commission ever since.

How have you done in sales?

I sold 230 cars my first year. I was rookie of the year, the number one new car salesperson in the Sewell organization of about a dozen dealerships and 100 plus salespeople. I was number eight in the whole Sewell dealership organization.

What kind of hours do you work?

I start between 7:30 and 8 a.m. I plan my day and make calls to prospects I've met as well as cold calls. It's best to get them early in the day when they are the freshest and give their attention to you. They get too busy after lunch. Often, there are people who arrive at the dealership early in the morning ready to buy cars, and not many salespeople are here in the morning. I try to leave between 6 and 7 p.m., but sometimes it's 8 or 9 p.m. I work five to six days a week, always on Saturday.

What is the environment like?

Lexus dealerships and Sewell dealerships are very nice places to work. Here in Texas it gets hot, and we try not to spend a lot of time on the lot, but you have to sometimes. It can be physically hard on people.

Where do you get names of people to call?

We have what we call an orphan list generated and managed by our business development center. We call people to tell them their previous salesperson is no longer at the dealership. We contact them a couple times during the year, calling them or sending cards and letters. Now, though, most of my business has been from referrals from other customers.

What do you like best about your job?

It's like having my own business. My success is dependent on me.

What is the worst part of your job?

People's perception of car salespeople. Folks have a perception of the old-fashioned, fast-talking car salesmen wearing the plaid sports coat. I just take it with a grain of salt and go on. I present myself to people professionally and show them I am here to help them. I try to establish early on what their needs and wants are. If you help people get what they want, everything will come your way.

Do you feel you have upward mobility?

Yes. Hopefully, I will move into management in new and pre-owned car sales. I could be a dealership general manager some day. There are lots of opportunities.

What kind of personality do you need to be a successful car salesperson?

You have to be high energy. You have to be a people person. You need to pay close attention to what customers are saying and focus on their needs.

What kind of education or training do you recommend?

If you sell luxury cars, you should have a college education because you will sell to highly educated people. But good work experience is the most important. I've received all kinds of on-the-job training that the dealership and Lexus have provided. I've learned a lot from other salespeople, including David Thomas, who is the number one Lexus salesman in the United States and works in our dealership.

Would you recommend a young person consider a career in car sales?

Yes. If they can deal with the long hours and hard work, it's a good career and you can make a good living.

Clay Schroff, 32
Salesman
Karl Malone Toyota
Albuquerque, New Mexico
Years in the business: six

How did you get into the car business?

I finished high school, then served in the military for four years. I worked mostly as a police officer. I got in the car business for a year, got out and went into radio advertising sales, then got back into the car business. There's nothing like it.

Do you like cars or have mechanical ability?

I pop the hood just to show buyers there's not a squirrel in there. I have very little interest in cars or mechanical things.

So why do you like selling cars?

Selling cars is not about the cars; it's about the people.

Why do you say that?

You meet such a variety of people. Everybody has a different need in a car, not to mention wants. They also have different financial situations. Some want to pay cash, some want to finance. Some have good credit, some have bad. So you first have to look at their needs and situation. Then you put them in a car that will make them happy during the time they own it. Your goal is to make them happy enough through the buying cycle that they say, "I won't deal with anybody else but Clay Schroff." If I did my best on the first sale, I always get the second sale.

What's the secret to your success?

I treat people well. The car business is starving for honest, hardworking salespeople. It doesn't take a lot to rise to the top. Every once in while, you may sacrifice a sale because the customer believes the guy down the street. I've had a lot of cases in which the person comes back to me six months after buying from a salesperson who wasn't honest and they are stuck with a car they don't want.

How many cars do you sell?

I sold 320 cars in 1998. I had the most sales in our group of 34 dealerships. I also helped manage the dealership for a couple of months.

How do you get customers?

Most are repeat buyers and referrals from satisfied customers. I don't make many cold calls anymore; I'm too busy. But when I was starting off, walk-ins and cold calls were important. The service department is a good place to find people to cold call. It sees thousands of people in a year, and they are people generally in one of our products already, so they are an easier sell.

What's your favorite part of the job?

I love being in my office putting the deal together and closing it. The more difficult the deal—not the customer, no one enjoys difficult customers—the more I enjoy it.

What's the least favorite part of your job?

Time away from my family, although it is better now. I now work only 45 to 50 hours per week, but I work weekends and special times of the year.

What kind of educational background or knowledge would you suggest someone have to go into car sales?

I'm not a good speller, and I have a hard time reading. But it's more important to be acquainted with what's going on in the world and your community—to have a finger on the pulse of what people are thinking.

What personality traits are important for success?

You need to be aggressive when people come in. If you are not the first to the customer who walks into the showroom or onto the dealership lot, you are not going to get the sale. You need to be disciplined to learn the product. You have to be willing to go out on the lot on hot days. When the customer says "no," it doesn't always mean "no." You need to ask for the sale and have the discipline to learn the product.

Have you had on-the-job training?

The dealership sends us to classes for product and motivational training. There is also training available in books and on tapes. I now train other individuals, and I learn more through training other people than going to a training session myself.

Is selling cars financially rewarding?

A good person in the car business can make $60,000 a year in their first year selling cars. When I got out of the military, I thought I would have no problem getting a high-paying job. But the unemployment office said without a college education I'd never make what I wanted to. And I've proven them wrong. I'm most proud of being the number one salesperson in our 34-dealership group. It's a thrill.

MECHANIC

If you spend every Saturday afternoon tinkering under the hood of your car, if you'd rather figure out for yourself what's making that knocking sound instead of paying someone else to, and if your friends tell you they don't trust anyone else but you to fix their car—then maybe you should consider turning your pastime into a profession.

As long as there are cars, there will be a need for people to fix them. But gone are the days of the "grease monkey" wielding a wrench. Automotive technology has become so complex that even backyard mechanics must take their cars to specialists for repairs and maintenance.

It is estimated that there are 775,000 automotive mechanics (or service technicians, as they're sometimes called) in the United States, but there's plenty of room for more. There will be even greater demand for mechanics in the future because more cars will be on the road and more people will try to keep their cars for longer periods of time.

Most mechanics work for automobile dealers, independent automotive repair shops, and gasoline service stations. With the increased complexity of the automobile, a mechanic frequently specializes in areas such as automatic transmissions, tune-ups, front ends, brakes, or air conditioning and heaters. Mechanics can also devote their practice to vehicles other than cars, such as diesel engine trucks, buses, motorcycles, or boats.

With thousands of car accidents guaranteeing a steady supply of work, some mechanics go into automotive body repair. They can specialize in this field as well, focusing on frame straightening or door and fender repairs, glass installation, fiberglass repair, or painting. Some workers especially enjoy customizing and refurbishing antique or "collector" cars.

You can break into the business with only a high school diploma and some body shop or automotive courses. Increasingly, however, employers are looking for formal training in automotive mechanics beyond high school.

If you like to hear the smooth purr of a well-tuned engine—and don't mind a little dirt under your fingernails—read on.

What You Need to Know

- ❏ Extensive knowledge of car mechanics and electronics
- ❏ Knowledge of computers (for diagnosing engine and electrical problems)
- ❏ Familiarity with tools
- ❏ Basic math (to calculate car repair costs)

Necessary Skills

- ❏ Mechanical know-how (ability to take apart objects with moving parts and put them back together again)
- ❏ Analytical skills (figuring out where a problem exists and how to solve it)
- ❏ Good communication skills (ability to talk to, ask questions of, and explain technical things to customers and service advisers)
- ❏ Knowledge of basic electronics

Do You Have What It Takes?

- ❏ Manual dexterity (ability to handle small tools and parts easily)
- ❏ Patience to deal with difficult or demanding customers
- ❏ Willingness to get your hands dirty
- ❏ Strong powers of observation (to eyeball which parts may not be functioning correctly)
- ❏ Ability to stick with a repair until it's finished

Education

A high school diploma is usually required. Auto repair courses (offered in vocational/technical schools or community colleges) are advisable. Automotive Service Excellence certification is a plus.

Getting into the Field

Licenses required

Driver's license

Job Outlook

Job openings will grow: much faster than average.
The supply of auto mechanics is far below the demand, so there are plenty of opportunities for mechanics who complete training programs.

The Ground Floor

Entry-level job: varies, depending on the training the person already has. The following jobs can lead to that of automotive mechanic:

❑ Porter or car washer. Helps prepare new and used cars for delivery and performs odd jobs within a dealership.
❑ Gasoline service attendant. Pumps gas, checks oil, performs minor repairs.
❑ Trainee, apprentice, or helper. Works with an experienced mechanic, shop foreman, or service manager. May lubricate cars and do light repairs.

On-the-Job Responsibilities

Beginners

❑ Wash cars
❑ Drive cars in and out of the service bay
❑ Lubricate cars
❑ Do light repairs and routine maintenance

Experienced Mechanics

❑ Talk with customer or service adviser about what is wrong with a car and what needs to be done
❑ Diagnose a problem based on information received from customer or service adviser, results of tests with tools such as infrared engine analyzers and computerized diagnostic devices, or a test drive of the car
❑ Provide a cost estimate of parts and labor needed to fix the problem
❑ Make adjustments and repairs, replacing parts that are broken or damaged

❑ Inspect car systems during routine maintenance checks

Automotive mechanics generally work 40 to 48 hours a week. Overtime may be necessary if there is a lot of work and/or a shortage of mechanics. Self-employed mechanics work longer hours. Mechanics usually start early in the morning, when most people drop off their cars for repair. Some dealerships and repair shops are open evenings and Saturdays. Mechanics usually have Sundays off.

All major holidays and one to four weeks of vacation a year, depending on the employer's policy.

❑ Retirement plan (about 20 percent of new car dealers offer a retirement plan)
❑ Manufacturer discounts on vehicles. Amount varies by manufacturer and the particular vehicle but is usually about five percent.
❑ Discounts on auto parts

❑ Dealerships for new and/or used cars
❑ Independent repair shops
❑ Gasoline service stations
❑ Automotive service facilities at department, automotive, and home-supply stores
❑ Companies maintaining fleets of cars and trucks, including rental car, taxicab, and automobile leasing companies
❑ Federal, state, and local governments
❑ Motor vehicle manufacturers
❑ Parts manufacturers and wholesalers

Beginners or experienced mechanics: little or no travel potential.

Employers sometimes send mechanics to factory training centers across the U.S. to learn to repair new models or to receive training in the repair of special components.

CARS

Surroundings

Mechanics work indoors most of the time, occasionally going out to test-drive a repaired car or to pick up or deliver a car. Modern repair shops are well lit and well ventilated, but the environment is often noisy because of all the equipment and are not usually air conditioned.

The work can be dirty and greasy, and minor cuts, burns, and bruises are common. The mechanic may have to get into awkward physical positions to repair hard-to-reach parts of the car. Some heavy lifting of parts and tools may be required. The mechanic must work with hazardous substances, including oil and transmission fluids, solvent, and paints. Some jobs require the use of special equipment, such as respirators for painting and goggles for welding.

On-the-Job Hazards

❑ Potential for injury because of lifting heavy parts and tools

❑ Minor cuts, burns, and bruises

Dollars and Cents

Weekly earnings of automotive mechanics who are wage and salary workers range from $250 to $1,000 per week, with a median salary of about $478. Many master mechanics earn from $70,000 to $100,000 annually. If you work overtime, you'll often earn a higher hourly wage. Mechanics with certification or those with a specialty earn more per hour.

Some dealerships and repair shops pay on a commission or profit-sharing basis so that the mechanic's weekly earnings depend on the amount of work completed. Some pay the mechanic a percentage of what the customer is charged. Under this arrangement, employers often guarantee a minimum weekly salary if commissions fall below the salary level.

Auto mechanics have tremendous opportunities for advancement. Experienced mechanics with strong leadership skills and good business sense can advance to shop supervisor or foreman, service manager, body shop manager, and general manager. A general manager can become an owner or co-owner of a dealership. A good mechanic always has the opportunity to open his own business. About one in five automotive mechanics today is self-employed.

Moving Up

Jobs are available across the U.S. Nearly every town has a dealership or repair shop that needs mechanics.

Where the Jobs Are

The best jobs go to automotive mechanics who complete a formal training program after high school. The post–high school training programs vary in length, from six months to two years, and usually include a combination of classroom instruction and hands-on experience. Training programs are offered by community colleges as well as public and private vocational and technical schools.

Automobile manufacturers and their participating dealers sponsor two-year associate degree programs in auto mechanics at community colleges across the country. The manufacturers provide equipment and cars for students to use for practice.

Voluntary certification—which can mean better pay and better jobs for a mechanic—is offered by the National Institute for Automotive Service Excellence. The certification is recognized as a standard of achievement for mechanics, body repairers, and painters. Mechanics are certified in one or more of eight different service areas, including electrical systems and engine repair. A master automotive mechanic is certified in all eight areas. Mechanics are retested every five years.

School Information

The vast majority of mechanics are men.

The Male/Female Equation

Making Your Decision: What to Consider

The Bad News

- ❏ "Grease monkey" job stereotype
- ❏ Skills require constant updating because of new techniques and equipment
- ❏ Regular exposure to hazardous chemicals
- ❏ Work can be dirty and greasy

The Good News

- ❏ Easy to break in
- ❏ Job security; career not likely to be affected by bad economy
- ❏ Satisfaction of seeing the results of your work
- ❏ Plentiful job opportunities

More Information Please

For information on training and certification for auto mechanics and auto body repairers or to obtain a list of certified schools for automotive mechanics and body repairers in your area, write:

National Institute for Automotive Service Excellence
13505 Dulles Technology Drive
Herndon, Virginia 22071–3415

For a directory of accredited private trade and technical schools that offer programs in automotive technician training, write:

Accrediting Commission of Career Schools
 and Colleges of Technology
2101 Wilson Boulevard, Suite 302
Arlington, Virginia 22201

WHAT IT'S REALLY LIKE

Marisol (Mary) Roman Yone, 38
Technician in training
Major Auto Group
Long Island City, New York
Years in the business: in training

What is your educational background?

I attended Bronx Community College in the evening. I studied medical technology, specializing in hematology. I eventually graduated with a degree in it, but what I really wanted all along was to major in automotive.

Why didn't you do that?

My mother, who was paying for my education, said automotive was a field for men. She said that I should go into medical technology, which she felt was better suited for women.

Were you always interested in cars?

As a child, I was interested in how cars were built and repaired. I loved seeing how junk cars could be made new again. In high school, I took an automotive class in vocational school and loved it.

How did you make the move to automotive?

While I was taking my medical technology courses, I was sneaking courses in automotive.

What automotive courses did you take?

I took physics, math, and chemistry. Then I also took courses on manual and automatic transmissions, brakes, front suspensions, electronics, painting, engine repair, and metal alignment. It took me ten years to get my associate degree in automotive technology.

Did those courses adequately train you for the job you are in now?

The college courses were mostly theoretical. We did have a little hands-on experience, but on older cars, so our knowledge was not up to date. There is a big difference between cars built in 1983 and those coming out for the year 2000. I'd say that was the only negative. Still, the hands-on experience was better than none at all.

Besides training and hands-on experience, what do you need to be a successful technician?

You have to be analytical. You need patience, self-confidence, and a sense of humor. You must not just like the trade but have a passion for it.

You are now working in the field as a trainee. How did you get that job?

It was difficult. I volunteered in a number of automotive shops in the Bronx. But they wouldn't hire me because I am a woman.

So this field is difficult for women to break into?

Yes. One guy told me I should go home and cook, not be in the automotive business. I was about ready to give up when I finally got my foot in the door here.

What are you doing as a trainee?

I am a trainee in general mechanics. I'll continue as a trainee until I become a full-fledged mechanic. They tried to get me to be a service adviser, but I turned down that offer because I love working on cars.

What do you most enjoy about your work?

I love taking something that is broken apart and putting it back together. I love seeing a car that had to be pushed into the garage out on the streets in running condition after I work on it.

What is your proudest professional achievement?

My proudest achievement is being able to get in the door in the automotive field. I'm also proud that I have been able to tackle everything they have given me without asking a lot of questions.

What is your ultimate goal?

I want to be the best female mechanic there is. That's my goal.

Scott Gregg, 39

Technician
Sewell Village Cadillac
Dallas, Texas
Years in the business: 20

Did you work on cars when you were a kid?

My dad was an electrical engineer, and he was always working on cars and other mechanical things at home. I grew up helping him. My dad bought me my first car, but I had to earn it by helping him overhaul the engine.

Did you take automotive courses in high school?

No. After I graduated from high school, I went to college for a year and hoped to get into veterinary medicine. I'd grown up on a farm and liked working with animals. But I couldn't face the seven years of college. I went to Lincoln Technical Institute, a two-year school for automotive.

What courses did you take?

The car was divided into different sections. We'd spend six weeks on each section, like the engine, transmission, air conditioning, and electrical systems.

How did you get your first job?

The school had a placement office, but I saw a help-wanted ad for an automotive mechanic at an Oldsmobile dealership. I applied for it and was hired. I was there for 10 years, then the dealership closed. The Sewell dealerships had been trying to recruit me for two to three years, even offering me a signing bonus. I told them I liked my job and would go with them when the dealership folded. I've now been with the Sewell group for nine years.

Do you do all kinds of repairs?

I do everything except for heavy engine repair and transmissions. We have departments that specialize in those because they are hard work and time-consuming jobs.

What is your schedule like?

I work 7:30 a.m. to 5 p.m. I work six days one week, including Saturday, and four the next.

What does supervising the other technicians involve?

I'm a group leader and supervise three other technicians. The service adviser works until 8 p.m. writing up reports on cars that are being checked in, so I review all the work that was written up the previous night as soon as I get in. I dispatch the jobs to the three technicians and myself. I start with vehicles that need diagnosis. That way the service adviser can get back to the customer to tell them what the problem is, the work that needs to be done, how much it will cost, and when it will be done. I also do the jobs that have specific promise times.

Do you receive extra pay for that?

Yes. I receive extra pay per hour for each technician I supervise. I check their diagnosis and look at their work when they are finished.

What kind of training or education would you recommend to people entering the field?

If they are going to work on General Motors cars, I'd suggest GM's Automotive Service Excellence program. The other manufacturers have similar programs. I worked with GM developing the curriculum, which is offered at junior colleges in most large cities. The student goes to school for 10 weeks, then works at a dealership for 10 weeks. The courses focus on GM products. I've found in training technicians that technical schools provide a basic knowledge but not the specific knowledge technicians need for certain car lines. It seems the people who have come out of these programs are more equipped to go to work than the people from technical schools. It takes them six months of working with me to get up to speed.

Do you have to keep up your training?

Yes. There are classes on new products, new engine, and new systems every year that we attend locally.

What kind of personality traits do you need to be a successful technician?

You need to be analytical. You need good technical skills. I have a lot of people come through who like cars and like working on them but don't have the technical skills. It's also best to be easygoing because tempers can flare. Good communication skills are important because you have to deal with the other technicians and get authorizations from managers and service advisers.

What is the biggest change you've seen in the automotive field since entering it?

The proliferation of electronics. They tell us that the 1999 Cadillac Seville, with its 19 computers, has more computers than the first lunar module that landed on the moon.

Are computer skills necessary for a technician?

Definitely. Not only are computers in the car, but the diagnostic tools are computers and even the service manual is on computer.

Does the computer make your job more difficult or easier?

It can go both ways. It's easier because the computers have self diagnostics and we use a scan tool to find out what's wrong. But sometimes there is a weird wiring problem or something, and it's a nightmare. What is happening on a car may have nothing to do with what is wrong with it.

Some technicians specialize in electronics. Do you recommend that?

I was a specialist in electronics for 14 years. But then I became a group leader and now do bumper-to-bumper repairs. Cars don't need as much maintenance these days. If someone specializes, they're not going to stay busy all the time. I'd suggest they have a broad range of skills.

Are there many jobs for technicians?

Yes. Technicians used to be a dime a dozen, but it's hard to find a good technician because cars are more sophisticated now. Dealerships are paying signing bonuses to steal technicians from other dealerships, like they did with me. A good, experienced technician can ask for anything.

So the pay is good?

Yes. And the hours aren't bad.

But the work can be physically demanding, right?

Yes. There's no air conditioning in the service area. And you are on your feet all day. I have problems with my ankles.

What is your long-term goal?

I have a standing offer for a management position within the dealership, but I make more money than managers and put in fewer hours. It's an option for when I'm older and more tired.

What are your proudest professional achievements?

I've won lots of awards. Technicians are measured through written tests, productivity, and the reject ratio of our repairs. I was a two-time Hall of Fame technician for Isuzu and won trips to Acapulco and California. I was the number one technician in the U.S. for Suzuki and won a trip to Paris for 10 days. I've been one of the top five Cadillac master craftsman technicians for two consecutive years and got cruises to the Virgin Islands. I've been an Oldsmobile master technician since 1984 and a master technician for Pontiac and GMC. Those awards include celebrations and prizes.

Tim Cacace, 40
Owner
Master Mechanix
Yonkers, New York
Years in the business: 26

Did you always have an interest in cars?
I've always had an interest in machines. I love working on things.

How did you get into the car repair business?
I went to an academic high school, so we did not have automotive courses. But we had seminars where local businessmen came to our school to talk about their fields. One was the owner of an auto repair business called Master Mechanix. After the seminar, I introduced myself. He said if I came by after school, he'd give me a job. I don't think I even had my driver's license yet, but I carried my tool box on the bus and went to work every day after school.

What did you do in that first job?
I was the low man on the totem pole. I pushed a broom around. Then they let me take a tire off. Then I learned to change oil. I got my sea legs.

Did you get more training?
My father insisted that I needed more training if I was going to survive in the business for the next 20 years. I

went to the State University of New York in Farmingdale, New York, for automotive technology. It was a two-year school, and I earned my associate's degree.

How did the training help you?

I gained an appreciation of the theory behind how things work and the theory of repairs. My course work was almost all theory and some lab. Half the people wanted more mechanical training, but I loved the theory because I already had three or four years of mechanical training under my belt.

Did you receive other training beyond your associate's degree?

I was one of the first mechanics certified by the ASE (Automotive Service Excellence) when it started its certification program.

What did you do after college?

I became a tradesman fixing heavy construction equipment. At 19, I was paid a huge salary and was responsible for a fleet of cranes, dump trucks, and other equipment.

How did you end up back at Master Mechanix?

After a couple years, I got laid off for a winter. I went back to visit my old boss. He said he was sick and tired of the business. I saw that as a door opening for me. He proposed that I take over the mechanical part of the business, and he would run the body shop. So at age 21, I took over a business.

Was that difficult?

I had to learn to manage people, and that was hard. Some of my employees were old enough to be my father.

How did your college training help?

The people who worked for me gained respect for me because I was able to figure out the tough problems. Sometimes when things go wrong with cars, no one can figure out what is wrong. So they need a diagnostician, and the guy who understands theory has an advantage. I had that from my schooling.

Did you eventually take over the entire business?

My former boss died, and I purchased the business from his family. I began the long process of modernizing the operation, which is still going on today. We have grown to fourteen employees.

Do you have difficulty finding technicians?

Always. The Grade A employees—those who have training and are certified in all fields certified by the ASE—are few and far between.

So how do you find technicians?

I teach nights at Bronx Community College, and I recruit my best students.

Why are there so few technicians?

We don't train auto mechanics properly in the United States. In Germany, they recruit promising young people from high schools and train them for seven years. They invest in them through apprenticeship programs. We've never had that kind of respect for the automobile mechanic in this country.

Is the image of the automobile mechanic a negative?

The automobile mechanic is always portrayed as the grease monkey or dope who can't do anything else so he's told to go fix cars. So many people who may have been inclined to enter the field have been discouraged by the image or by their parents who tell them there is no respect in it. Unfortunately, the field then attracts kids in high school who can't produce and wind up in automotive mechanics by default. Because cars have become so sophisticated, this is a challenging field. For example, I teach students about anti-lock brakes. That requires an understanding of digital circuitry.

Are there any other down sides to being an automotive mechanic?

You need to get experience, but to gain experience, you need to have tools. The typical mechanic has $30,000 to $40,000 in tools and constantly makes investments in new tools. Also, you get dirty every day. Sometimes you have to lie on the ground or in snow to see under a car. And customers are always upset with us. When their car doesn't perform the way they think it should, it is always the mechanic's fault because he's first in the line of fire.

Is the pay good?

Wages have not caught up to where they should be compared with the plumbing and electrical trades. It will take five years before a student is earning $800 to $1000 a week. And many small independent shops do not pay benefits or sick days or provide uniforms.

Isn't that changing with the intense shortage of technicians?

Yes. We're starting to see mechanics being offered starting pay of $75,000 with sign-on bonuses. Some companies, like BMW, are paying relocation expenses. GM and Ford have begun training and recruiting from high schools.

How does a student get experience and a job?

Some high schools and colleges offer training programs. Students should try to get a referral from someone on the faculty to a business owner in the community. I've developed a network of about 10 shops through the college and the radio show I participate in who ask for names of students. Open any newspaper and answer an ad to try to break in.

What qualities does someone need to be a good automotive technician?

A person needs to be patient, analytical, and logical. Good communication skills and an ability to get along with customers and fellow employees are important too.

Is the field as open to women as men?

I've had a couple women mechanics. Unfortunately, it is a harsh environment with long hours—10 hours a day or more and Saturdays. And the male mechanics can be tough on the female mechanics. As an owner, I can't control that all of the time.

What is your proudest professional achievement?

I've had 20 years of success owning a business. I've made it; a lot of guys don't. I'm now being recognized for that achievement through the call-in radio show program I participate in. I've gained the reputation as someone who helps people with problems.

CLAIMS REPRESENTATIVE

As the saying goes, "Accidents will happen." And when they do, an auto claims representative is never far behind. It's his or her job to decide how much money people are entitled to receive on their insurance claim after a car accident. Although the procedure is always the same, the people and events never are.

A claim may be filed after a simple fender bender, or there may be extensive damage and serious injury, even death. And sometimes an accident may not be an accident at all, but a fraud.

There is a variety of jobs within the field. As an auto claims representative or adjuster, you determine whether losses or damages from an auto accident are covered by the insurance company's policies. If they are, you estimate the costs of the repair or replacement. Then you work out a settlement that is fair to both the policyholder and the insurance company. You negotiate with the auto body repair shop or dealership to have the work done at the price the insurance company is willing to pay.

If there are injuries or a death that result from an auto accident, the auto claims adjuster may be involved in gathering medical reports and often communicates with a bodily injury adjuster, who settles medical claims.

Adjusters spend half of their time talking with policyholders, investigating claims, and, in the case of outside adjusters, visiting dealerships and auto body repair shops.

The other half of the adjuster's time is spent filling out the required forms and filing reports, more often than not on a computer.

An inside auto claims adjuster works primarily from an office, while an outside adjuster spends a great deal of time at various locations investigating claims. A technical specialist claims adjuster does the job of an inside or outside adjuster but is involved in more complex and technical work.

The adjuster may be aided by an auto damage appraiser, who looks over the physical damage to a car to determine the approximate cost of repairs. Based on the appraiser's cost estimates, the adjuster then places a value on the claim and negotiates a settlement.

Adjusters and appraisers work for property liability insurance companies or for independent companies that examine accidents for insurance companies.

No one is ever happy to have a car accident, but those involved can be helped through their inconvenience or distress by a claims representative who does his or her job well. If you like automobiles and also enjoy figuring out an occasional mystery, this career could suit both your interests.

What You Need to Know

- ❑ Basic knowledge of how insurance works
- ❑ Basic auto mechanics and auto body repair techniques (what's necessary and what repairs cost)

Necessary skills

- ❑ Ability to negotiate a settlement that makes business sense for your company and satisfies the policyholder
- ❑ Basic computer know-how (most representatives now use computers to do their paperwork and to communicate with their main office)
- ❑ Good listening skills and notetaking know-how (you need to accurately record everything witnesses or policyholders tell you)
- ❑ Ability to ask questions, listen carefully, and put together what you observe with what you hear from the policyholder.

Do You Have What It Takes?

- ❑ A sense of objectivity that allows you to make professional judgments, regardless of the details of the accident or the persuasiveness of the policyholder or auto repair specialists
- ❑ Ability to remain calm when policyholders or repair specialists become difficult
- ❑ A good eye; you need to carefully observe damage

Education

A high school diploma is required. An associate degree is preferred.

Licenses Required

Companies provide new claims adjusters and examiners with on-the-job training and home-study courses or send them to courses offered by the Insurance Institute of America, a nonprofit organization offering educational programs to professionals in the field. Their courses prepare adjusters and examiners for the licensing tests required in many states. To apply for a license, you must do one or more of the following: pass a written exam, complete approved course work, furnish character references, and/or be at least 20 years of age and a resident of the state in which you're working.

Job Outlook

Job openings will grow: faster than average.

The strongest demand is for auto claims representatives who know auto body shop procedures.

The Ground Floor

Entry-level job: Auto claims assistant

This clerical job can help prepare you to become a full-fledged adjuster.

Not everyone starts as an auto claims assistant; people with auto body repair experience may start as full-fledged adjusters.

On-the-Job Responsibilities

Beginners (auto claims assistant)

❏ Answer initial telephone calls from policyholders on how to file a claim
❏ Take information on new claims and open a file for the adjuster
❏ Make appointments for an inspection by the adjuster
❏ Keep policyholders informed on the status of pending claims

Senior Assistants

❏ Do all the above, plus handle minor claims

Experienced Adjusters

❏ Investigate claims by interviewing people involved in an accident and any witnesses
❏ Examine police reports of the accident
❏ Estimate amount of damage to the car
❏ Determine who is at fault in the accident

❏ Decide if the insurance policy covers the claim
❏ Negotiate a settlement on the claim with the policyholder
❏ Negotiate with adjusters from other insurance companies on claims that involve their policyholders
❏ Authorize payment on the claim

Some insurance companies also hire auto damage appraisers, whose main responsibility is to determine the approximate cost of repairs.

Auto claims representatives generally work nine to five, Monday through Friday. Some adjusters have the flexibility to arrange their work schedules to meet policyholders on evenings or weekends. Some insurance companies offer or are experimenting with work-at-home opportunities, flextime, and part-time positions.

When You'll Work

All insurance companies offer one to three weeks of paid vacations as well as holidays off.

Time Off

❏ Pension plan
❏ Tuition reimbursement for course work related to the job
❏ Company car or payment for use of personal car. Adjusters who work for the insurance companies owned by General Motors, Ford Motor Company, and DaimlerChrysler AG receive company cars.

Perks

❏ Auto insurance companies
❏ Independent insurance appraisers

Who's Hiring

Beginners: No travel potential

Experienced outside adjusters: Some local travel.

Places You'll Go

They travel to conduct investigations and visit auto body shops. How much time is spent traveling depends on the size of their assigned territory and the number of adjusters working in that area. An adjuster in a rural area may be required to drive longer distances because the area covers many square miles. An adjuster in a large claims office in an urban area may only drive to a small section of the city because the work is shared by a number of adjusters and the territory is small, though heavily populated.

Surroundings

Auto claims representatives work in pleasant offices. Outside claims adjusters spend up to half of their time away from the office in varied locales, such as tow yards, auto body repair shops, and car dealerships.

Dollars and Cents

Salaries range from $24,000 to $42,000 per year.

Moving Up

With experience and additional on-the-job training or home-study course work in insurance, an auto claims representative has excellent potential for advancing to jobs such as claims supervisor and claims examiner.

The claims supervisor is responsible for the investigation and settlement of all claims assigned to the department. Some offices also have a claims manager who is a level above supervisor. A claims examiner manages the settlement of complex, high-value claims and gives technical direction to adjusters. A well-established claims adjuster can also transfer from the auto field to handling marine or industrial claims or those brought on by a natural disaster.

In some companies a four-year degree is helpful for advancing into managerial positions.

Where the Jobs Are

Jobs are available in nearly every area of the country, although they are more plentiful in major metropolitan areas where there is a concentration of cars, accidents, and claims offices.

Training

Insurance companies often provide on-the-job classroom training in company procedures and policies. Many pay for courses provided by the Insurance Institute of America, a nonprofit organization offering educational programs and professional certification. The Institute offers an Associate in Claims designation after a person successfully completes four areas of course work and examinations in various types of claims adjusting.

Participants can prepare for the exams through independent home study, courses provided through the company, or classes held at a public location such as a college campus or public meeting room.

The field of auto claims is open equally to men and women, but it is more populated by men.

The Male/Female Equation

Making Your Decision: What to Consider

The Bad News

- ❏ Substantial paperwork
- ❏ Lack of variety in job tasks for inside adjusters
- ❏ Some companies set high quotas of cases to be handled
- ❏ Clients can be difficult, and difficult to please

The Good News

- ❏ Regular working hours
- ❏ Good pay, above-average benefits
- ❏ Potential for advancement with additional training and education
- ❏ Job security; industry unaffected by ups and downs of the economy

To receive a brochure on careers in the property and casualty insurance industry, write or call:

The Insurance Information Institute
110 William Street
New York, New York 10038
212-669-9200

More Information Please

Insurance Institute of America
720 Providence Road
P.O. Box 3016
Malvern, Pennsylvania 19355-0716
610-644-2100
Web site: http://www.aicpcu.org

WHAT IT'S REALLY LIKE

Shari Summers, 44
Account Manager
General Motors Corp.—Motors Insurance Corp.
Newhall, California
Years in the business: 26

How did you get into the auto insurance business?

During my last months of high school, I worked part-time at a Los Angeles–area branch of General Motors' Motors Insurance Corp. (MIC). Eventually, I moved to a number of departments, including accounting and the computer room.

What did you do in the claims department?

I was a claims examiner. Unlike the claims adjusters, I didn't inspect the vehicles prior to the repair but looked at the repair orders after the work was performed. My job was to communicate with the outside adjusters who were looking at the damaged vehicles, and, as the in-office adjuster, I authorized the repair work.

What does your current job as account manager involve?

As an account manager, I have a base of thirty-three dealers I call on. I'm responsible for making sure they know how to do repairs, what is covered by the warranty agreement, and how claims should be submitted and prices set. Out in the field, I look at what repairs were done and make sure they were done properly. Occasionally, I inspect parts that were replaced.

What do you do if the repair is not done properly?

I counsel the dealership on doing the repair properly. In some cases, I collect back some of the money we've paid them.

Do you work in an office?

After 20 years in an office, I now have an office in my home. I sometimes miss the camaraderie of fellow workers, but I don't miss the office politics. Besides, I spend most of my time at my thirty-three dealerships.

How much do you travel?

I have one dealer group 200 miles away. I spend one week a month in central California calling on those dealers. I also have four dealers in Hawaii, so I go there every three or four months.

What is a typical week like?

I might spend a couple of full days at one dealership, pulling service files, reviewing the claims that were paid, and making sure the dealership followed guidelines. I'll discuss proper procedures with the dealership personnel. That may require a couple days in a conference room at one dealership.

Another day, I may visit three dealers in a certain area, spending a few hours at each dealership, helping the personnel with questions or problems like submission of claims. Or the service advisers might ask me questions. I'll also talk to the people who sell the GM Protection Plan to customers. I deal with everybody at the dealership, from the dealer to the clerks.

What do you do in your home office?

I do paperwork. I use the phone or work on the computer to try to resolve problems on claims payments.

Do you like cars?

I have always liked cars. Liking cars is not a necessity for this job, but going to a dealership and intelligently understanding what's wrong with an engine helps you gain the trust of the dealer.

What do you like best about your job?

I like my current job because I am empowered and free to make the decisions I feel are necessary. I am not second-guessed. I also make my own schedule. I decide who to see and when I'll go to a dealership and what day will be an office day.

What's the worst part about your job?

I'm buried in paperwork. It requires being very organized, but I still get frustrated and overwhelmed with it.

What education or training have you received?

I've had different kinds of training, some at mechanical schools and professional contact skills schools. I've taken courses on how to handle difficult people and angry customers.

What kind of personality do you need to be in insurance claims?

You must be a people person. You need to be able to walk in, sit down, and start chitchatting with a dealer. This qualification is less important for outside claims adjusters who study accidents and schedule repairs. You have to be very organized and very motivated because you are on your own. You must have negotiation skills and be willing to back down when you are wrong and be assertive when you know you are right. You need a good understanding of your product.

Are mechanical skills necessary?

Having mechanical skills helps. I have a friend who is in claims who doesn't know much about the mechanical aspects, and it hurts her. She went to school and it helped make her more confident. I helped my husband overhaul a boat engine. He always keeps me involved in mechanical projects he is working on.

I've learned that when I don't understand something mechanical to ask for an explanation or ask to be shown what they mean. To try to make a dealer, for instance, think you know something when you don't makes you look foolish.

What other skills are useful?

Good writing skills are very important.

What advice would you give young people entering the field?

I'd tell them the same as I tell everyone—the more education you have, the better.

Is the field as open to women as men?

Yes. In California, we have the same number of women account managers as men, though that isn't true across the country. It's always been harder for women to break in as adjusters, but that's changing with the new generation of management.

Is there much upward mobility and opportunities across the country?

I'm lucky to have made it to where I am. I could have moved up more with more education or a degree. And I could have moved anywhere in the United States; MIC has offices everywhere. I've done such completely different jobs at GMAC for 26 years that it feels like I've worked for different corporations.

Rick Marsh, 50
Auto Reinspector
The Chubb Group Insurance
Floram Park, New Jersey
Years in the business: 22

How did you get into the claims area?
I started working at a dealership, where I later became a body shop manager. While I was there, I took a training course on estimating with Chubb. When the dealership was sold, I went to work for Motor Club Insurance from 1977 to 1980. Then I went to work for Chubb. It is a good solid company with 401K and benefits. I've been here for 19 years.

What jobs have you held at Chubb?
First I was hired as an outside staff appraiser, estimating how much repairs would cost. Then I was a reinspector. My job was to check the quality of claims to make sure estimates were being adhered to. For the last four years, I've been a zone reinspector. I check the quality of the claims and estimates for an entire geographic region.

What preparation did you have for your current job?
Chubb sends its employees to courses. I've taken a course on collision repair. We actually went to Montreal and watched the new repairs being done. Cars and the repair business change so much you have to take new courses every five years or so.

What changes have you seen in the industry?
Chubb has gone to independent appraisers who are paid by Chubb to do the appraisals but are not employees of Chubb.

How have computers changed the industry?
Twenty years ago, we had to use a Polaroid camera to document the damage and submit a lot of paperwork on the damage and the estimates for repairs. Today, we use digital cameras and transmit the images via the computer to a central office. And we enter a VIN (Vehicle Identifi-

cation Number) into a computer to get all the information we need about the accident, the damage, the parts needed for repair, and the cost for repairs and labor. Computers eliminate the time it took to look things up and get in touch with various offices. Now all claims are processed through a central office.

How has technology made you more productive?

Details concerning the percentages of paint, parts, labor, and time are calculated by the computer and reduced in half the time it takes to do an estimate. I'll get a fax of a claims estimate. I inspect the quality of the estimate. I'll make a report within 24 to 48 hours authorizing the repairs. My job now is to make sure the independent appraisers are doing quality adjustments and keep up with Chubb standards.

What is a typical day or week like on the job?

I try to schedule a certain number of claims each day for review. It is difficult to schedule a day, but I try to have a pattern. There could be a complaint for re-inspection that needs to be done quickly. When I am on the road doing claims, I try to make a circle in a concentrated area. I come inside to do reports and prepare backgrounds regarding disputes between insurance carriers as to who will pay and how much will be paid. I explain our side of it to a panel of three arbiters. We look at supporting documents, make decisions about who is at fault and determine negligence.

Do you spend a lot of time on the road?

I have a workstation at home with access to everything I have in the office. I can review files, look up histories, and make comments. Sometimes I don't go into the office for weeks. I have a laptop and access to information wherever I go. I go out to shops to see new equipment and state-of-the-art tools to do repairs on newer cars. Those costs can be incredibly expensive.

What do you like about your job?

I like the independence of working away from a desk and working outside. It is not humdrum like working on an assembly line. There is something new every day. And I enjoy meeting new people. I get paid very well for what I do. It is still rewarding to see a finished product every time I do an estimate.

What skills and personality traits does a person need to be an insurance claims representative?

You do not necessarily need a body shop or mechanical background. If you have negotiating skills and are self motivated, this field is a good choice. It helps to have some basic computer skills.

What has brought you the most job satisfaction?

I'm proud of going from adjuster to zone supervisor. And it is a pleasure to do a job well and properly all the time. If cars are not repaired properly, it costs more money to repair them a second time.

Linda Gardner, 49
Claims Specialist
Safeco
Stone Mountain, Georgia
Years in business: 23

How did you get into the insurance business?

I have a degree in elementary education and taught for about a year and a half before I quit to raise my son. When I decided to work part-time, I went through a temporary help agency. I went to work for the Reserve Insurance Company in Atlanta as a capture claims processor, and moved up to become an adjuster.

What was your next job?

I went to work for Sentry Insurance Company as a claims adjuster and became the claims unit manager. I handled simple claims, no- fault insurance claims, and medical bills for insured customers injured in accidents. They did not involve a lot of investigation. I did not become involved in larger claims.

What did you do next?
I went to work as a paralegal for an insurance defense attorney who defended claims for insurance companies. After four years in that job, I came back to work for Safeco as a claims specialist. Because I have always been interested in medical and legal things, I developed expertise in those areas.

What is a typical day or week like on the job?
My job involves a variety of things, from handling a simple fender bender to handling claims that have death or catastrophic injury. The majority of my work is done in the office. Sometimes I take a file home and work on it. I spend about five to ten percent of my time on the road.

How have computers changed your job?
We are doing more of our work on computer. We are moving toward a paperless environment.

What kind of training have you added since you became an adjuster?
I have taken courses at outside seminars conducted by attorneys and medical groups. Some of it I did on the job, researching specific cases from medical and legal view points. I got an associate claim degree from Insurance Institute of America. I also got its certificate in general insurance—both while working for insurance companies. I also get a lot of in-house training. Attorneys come in and update us on changes in the law and medical field.

What do you like best about your job?
I like the larger cases with medical and legal issues that I can delve into and research from different angles. I enjoy working with people on the outside and in the office. Sometimes it can be a challenge to make people happy.

What do you dislike about the job?

Really, there is nothing I don't like. I can't imagine doing anything else.

What advice would you give to someone interested in being a claims representative?

It can be a fun job. Some days are routine, but there are opportunities if you are willing to take advantage of them.

What kind of education or training would you recommend?

Consider getting into risk management, which you can take courses in at business schools. It's a good background. You'll learn insurance contracts and exposures as well as an overview of the industry. Then you can go into any insurance field and have a basic understanding of the business.

What is your proudest achievement in this field?

I guess it is not one particular file, but several complex files that involved complicated medical and liability issues. I found information by doing research and following up to put the pieces together. I was able to amass a set of facts to get a fair settlement for everyone involved.

ELECTRONICS SPECIALIST

If you're a tinkerer and prefer electronic over mechanical equipment, consider a career as an electronics specialist. You can be a robot doctor— the technician people call when they need someone to troubleshoot problems that arise on the assembly line and throughout the factory. Getting specialized training is a must, but the payoff in salary makes this job rewarding.

The assembly plants that produce motor vehicles and the parts that go into them are increasingly filled with automated and electronic equipment that has to be installed and maintained by electronics specialists.

An electronics specialist in the auto industry performs a wide variety of jobs, from repairing light fixtures in an assembly plant to programming the robots that install windshields into cars and trucks. They usually work in manufacturing plants that make cars and trucks or the parts to go in them. However, some jobs are in office buildings and research laboratories where automotive electronic equipment is developed and tested.

Electronics specialists in factories install and maintain the electronic equipment on the assembly line, including the robots that weld and paint the cars, install the windshields, and apply sealant material around the doors. Driverless automated guided vehicles carry parts and partially built vehicle bodies to the assembly line. Other electronic equipment diagnoses problems in the vehicles and insures quality control.

Electronics specialists maintain the equipment but may be called upon to work with manufacturing and automation engineers to check out new equipment that they intend to install in the plant. They then install it, program it, and teach assembly line workers how to use it properly. They also provide advice on how to improve the productivity of the plant. When a quality problem occurs in vehicles, electronics specialists are asked to figure out where the problem occurred on the assembly line and fix it.

Some electronics specialists focus on the maintenance of the plant itself instead of the assembly line. Keeping a plant in tip-top running condition is critical, so plants are constantly updating their facilities. The electronics specialist is involved in the upkeep of existing facilities, the construction of additions, and renovations of existing space.

The electronics specialist is typically required to go through an apprenticeship program, which involves classroom training and on-the-job experience. A beginning apprentice will perform chores as mundane as changing lighting fixtures and installing electrical receptacles. With experience, an electronics specialist can advance to more sophisticated tasks, such as troubleshooting scientific machinery in the laboratory or programming robots on the assembly line.

What You Need to Know

- ❏ Knowledge of electricity and how electronic equipment works
- ❏ Basic knowledge of computers
- ❏ Solid math, science, and reading skills

Necessary Skills

- ❏ Ability to use tools, such as voltmeters and oscilloscopes, used in electronics
- ❏ Ability to take apart and put back together electronic equipment
- ❏ Ability to work carefully and precisely

Do You Have What It Takes?

- ❏ Drive to improve existing processes and equipment
- ❏ Patience to search for a solution to a problem
- ❏ Interest in acquiring new skills
- ❏ Personality to work with others to get a job done

Physical Qualities

- ❏ Manual dexterity (to handle tools and parts easily)
- ❏ Good eyesight and color vision

Education

A high school diploma is required. An apprenticeship is also required and may include work on an assembly line or in plant maintenance. Employers prefer an associate degree in engineering technology. As technology becomes more sophisticated, employers will look for technicians who are skilled in new technologies and have obtained additional job training.

Licenses Required

A license to perform electrical work is required. Other certifications may be required through the company-union apprenticeship programs.

Getting Into The Field

CARS

Job Outlook

Job openings will grow: as fast as average. Large numbers of retirements are expected, so new openings will become available.

The Ground Floor

Entry-level job: assembly line worker, plant maintenance, or apprentice

On-The-Job Responsibilities

Beginners

- ❏ Change light fixtures
- ❏ Install electric receptacles
- ❏ Assist and observe experienced electronics specialists in installing, programming, and maintaining automated and electronic equipment
- ❏ Participate in classroom training

Experienced Employees

- ❏ Install automation on the assembly line
- ❏ Maintain automated and electronic equipment on the assembly line
- ❏ Test automated equipment
- ❏ Develop new equipment in a scientific laboratory
- ❏ Troubleshoot electronic equipment problems on the assembly line

When You'll Work

Engineering specialists work round-the-clock to handle problems and maintenance of assembly line equipment. Overtime is often required when bugs are being worked out of new equipment, a new vehicle is launched, a specific project like construction of a plant addition is nearing deadline, or plants are running full speed to meet strong marketplace demands.

Time Off

Large companies employing engineering specialists offer major holidays off, sick time, and two to three weeks of paid vacation. Vacations may be specified at certain times of the year when factories are closed for the Christmas holiday or summer shutdown.

❑ Pension plans

❑ Health-care insurance

❑ Stock purchase plans are offered by General Motors Corporation, Ford Motor Company, and DaimlerChrysler as well as some large auto parts companies. (In such plans, for every share purchased by the employee, the company buys a share or part of a share for that employee.)

❑ Tuition reimbursement for college courses in engineering, engineering technology, or business management

❑ Auto manufacturers

❑ Most large auto parts manufacturers

Beginners and experienced workers: little or no travel potential.

More experienced workers may be able to transfer to a company's other plants.

Electronics specialists in the auto industry generally work in a manufacturing plant. No longer like the dark and dingy plants of the past, today's manufacturing facilities generally are clean and well lit. They are noisy and busy. The electronics specialist typically is on the move, working in various parts of the plant.

❑ Danger of electrical shock (if you're not careful)

❑ Noisy environment can damage hearing

Salaries start at around $20,200. More experienced engineering specialists earn an average of $32,700, and those in supervisory or senior level position make about $54,800 a year. Overtime pay can add up substantially. Some experienced electronics specialists can make $100,000 a year in strong auto sales years.

Moving Up

Where The Jobs Are

Training

The Male/Female Equation

Making Your Decision: What To Consider

More Information Please

Electronics specialists can move up to supervisory positions with experience and additional training.

Most jobs for electronics specialists in auto plants are in the Midwest.

Major automobile manufacturers offer apprenticeship programs. Labor unions representing electrical workers also provide apprenticeship programs. The training for both includes classroom work as well as hands-on experience under the guidance of experienced electrical specialists.

The field is dominated by men, although it is open to women.

The Bad News

- ❏ Shift work
- ❏ Cyclical auto industry lays off workers in slow sales periods
- ❏ Factory work is noisy and can be dirty
- ❏ Continued education and training required

The Good News

- ❏ Good pay
- ❏ Above-average benefits
- ❏ Skills transfer to other manufacturing and electronic fields
- ❏ Opportunity to acquire new skills at employer's expense
- ❏ Potential for advancement

For a small fee, you can get a package of information from:

The Junior Engineering Technical Society
1420 King Street, Suite 405
Alexandria, Virginia 22314-2794

Information on ABET-accredited engineering technology programs is available from:

Accreditation Board for Engineering and Technology, Inc.
111 Market Place, Suite 1050
Baltimore, Maryland 21202

What It's Really Like

Ed Dearnley, 46
Electronics Specialist
General Motors Corporation
Warren, Michigan
Years in the business: 26

How did you get into the automotive industry?

I graduated from high school and went to Michigan State University for two semesters. In 1973, I was hired as a general assembler for the Cadillac Motor Car Division and began working on the assembly line.

Did you get into the business because you liked cars?

No. In fact, I don't work on my own cars. I got into the business because it was a good job.

Are you mechanically inclined?

When I started, I had no mechanical skills. Once I tore a lawn mower apart and had to buy a new one because I couldn't put it back together. When I started the apprenticeship, I got gutsy. I wanted to try fixing things. Over 26 years, I have become mechanically inclined. I like to see how things work and try to figure out why things fail.

How did you make the move into the skilled trades?

In 1979, I applied for a skilled trade apprenticeship. General Motors has an apprenticeship program that you can apply to as soon as you are hired. I took a series of tests and went through interviews. I wanted to get into Cadillac engineering so I wouldn't be doing repetitious assembly line work. I also wanted to work in a better environment with air conditioning and earn more money.

What did the apprentice program involve?

It remains today as it was when I was in it. It is a four-year program that included classes at night and hands-on training during the work week. I rotated through different jobs within the engineering facility. I'd work on the total vehicle for a month, transmissions for another month, engines the next month. I rotated through the facility until I'd achieved all the hours I needed. I ended up as an experimental assembler, which is somewhat like a mechanic except that you don't just fix things that are broken but take existing parts and make them fit on future vehicles for prototypes.

What kind of classes did you take?

I went to Macomb Community College at night, where I took drafting, math, mechanical reasoning, space relations, and blueprint reading. With my two semesters at Michigan State, my classes at Macomb, and credit from my apprenticeship, I earned an associate degree.

What did you do after you finished the apprenticeship?

I went to Cadillac engineering where I worked in the garage on future products. I worked on the whole car, not just the transmission or engine, which is why I picked it. But that lasted only a couple of weeks. Then I was appointed to an eight-man team that Cadillac had formed to handle service calls from dealers with problems with the electronics. Cadillac had just opened a new assembly plant that was building Cadillacs, Oldsmobiles, and Buicks. They were the earliest cars to have extensive electronics. They had miles and miles of wiring and lots of communication between electronic modules. For three years, I helped the technicians at dealerships by phone, or I'd go to the dealership.

What was your next job?

The electronics in the cars improved to the point that our team was disbanded. Because I had gained so much knowledge, I moved into the area of durability and validation of vehicles that were being developed. We did cold weather testing in northern Canada in the winter and hot weather testing in Phoenix in the summer. My job was to provide daily reports to the engineers on how the cars were operating, the problems that occurred, and what the root causes of the problems were. We were responsible for the total car, but the electronics were the most challenging.

What is your current job?

I'm in a temporary assignment in the General Motors' division that builds midsize and luxury cars. I'm the electronics specialist involved in tearing down future vehicles, reworking them and putting them back together.

What skills are necessary to become an electronics specialist?

You need troubleshooting skills. With electronics, you may think something is working correctly, but it may not be.

How do you know that something is not right?

We use voltmeters, which check for an electrical charge, and oscilloscopes, which show the frequency of the charge. But the computer has been the most important tool we use. The laptop computer allows us to monitor the computers onboard the car.

How did you learn about computers?

I picked up computer classes here at General Motors. I learned Lotus Notes, Windows, and Excel. These are tools we use to communicate internally at General Motors with engineers, designers, and people in manufacturing. I also took a class from a supplier to General Motors on using the laptop computer to take a snapshot of the data inside the car—basically to learn to communicate with the car.

Why do you prefer electronic over mechanical work?

I like tackling more difficult problems. Mechanical things are easy to figure out. You can see something turn this way and understand why it happens. With electronics, you push a button and something happens, but you can't see why it happens. It takes more effort to find out how it works, or why it is not working.

How has the technology of cars changed since you went through your apprenticeship?

The electronics technology has grown by leaps and bounds. In 1986, there were three computers on board the car. Today, a car can be loaded with twenty computers. Meanwhile, the mechanical elements are basically the same as they have been for many years.

What personality traits does a person need to be successful at a skilled trade?

People skills are necessary. I didn't have them in the beginning; I was shy. I needed them to communicate effectively with engineers. I needed them to handle service calls from dealers when I was on the Cadillac team specializing in the new automotive electronics. I also had to give presentations and provide training on electronics to people inside the company and at dealerships throughout the country. My job was to pass on what we had learned to mechanics at dealerships to make their lives easier when they were troubleshooting a car. I had to speak before 50 to 400 people at times. I did fine speaking when I knew the subject thoroughly.

What most excites you about working in this field?

My favorite part is when I learn something new. Doing the same thing day in and day out is not for me. But throw me something new, and I'm excited.

Eddie Robison, 42
Team Leader
Toyota Motor Manufacturing, Inc.
Georgetown, Kentucky
Years in the business: 12

How did you get into involved in the automotive industry?
I was working construction and traveling around the country a lot on projects when I first applied to Toyota. Toyota built an assembly plant in Georgetown, Kentucky, in 1986; in 1988, it began production of the Toyota Camry.

Were you interested in automobiles?
I was interested in a good-paying, permanent job, and I wanted to spend more time with my family.

What is your job at Toyota?
I'm in the facilities control department. We maintain all of the building equipment from the heating, ventilation, and air conditioning to the high voltage power system, security systems, and hand-held radios.

Do you have jobs related directly to the production of the vehicles?
On the assembly line, we are responsible for the final inspection and calibration of the equipment. We set the front- and rear-end alignments of the cars. We make sure all of the automobile's safety equipment is working. We adjust the headlights. We do the final tuning of the engines.

What training did you have for this job?
I attended four years of vocational-technical training, specializing in electricity. I went through a four-year apprenticeship with the International Brotherhood of Electrical Workers. And I took several training classes through Toyota's training center. I took all of the electrical classes.

Have you taken computer classes?

I've taken several. I've also taken programming courses because I write some of the programs we use.

How do you use computers in your work?

In my day-to-day work, I use a computerized maintenance management system. I enter data into it. I coordinate with the rest of the department to make sure everything is done.

This morning I made modifications to one of the programs I wrote. I entered the work that I will perform today. The program also has a history of the equipment, its maintenance, and how many man-hours each piece of equipment was worked on so we can track costs.

What skills do people need to do your job?

The skills required are becoming more technical all the time. Good computer knowledge is essential. Also, hand coordination is necessary for working with tools.

What personality traits do you need to be successful?

I came here primarily as an electrician. Now I have multiple skills. That's what employers like Toyota are looking for. You must have a willingness to learn new things. You need to be self-motivated and organized.

What's the best part of your job?

I have the ability to direct my own work. I have a set of jobs I need to get done, but it's up to me to determine what I do and when. Not all jobs are like mine, however. I enjoy fooling with the computers and programs.

What's the least favorite part of your job?

Paperwork.

What advice would you give young people entering your field?

If they really want to get into the area I'm in, I feel they need to get some job training. They need experience in the work world. I've worked with a lot of students coming out of college. They have good ideas, but they don't know how to implement them because they've never been in the workforce.

What is the most rewarding part of your work?

What fulfills me most either with a program or a special project is when it's finished and somebody tells me I've done a good job. I did a major project last year renovating a building to be a parts area. It took nearly five months. Several people from different groups commended me on the success of the project.

Henry Zukow, 59
Electronics Training Specialist
Huron Technical Training Center,
Ford Motor Company
Ypsilanti, Michigan
Years in the business: 33

Were you always interested in cars?

My high school buddies and I always played around with our cars. But I took college-prep courses in high school, not mechanical courses.

How did you get in the automotive industry?

I worked at a marina for several years as a mechanic, then switched to motorcycles. A friend suggested I go to work for Ford Motor Company where I would not be laid off in the winter and I'd have good benefits. I went right into the apprenticeship program.

What did the apprenticeship program involve?

The Ford apprenticeship program remains much as it was when I enrolled and is one of largest in the country. I was in the four-year electrical apprenticeship. You have to put in so many hours of work time and roughly 500 hours of classroom time. Classes include math, drawing, electrical circuits, and motors. You are paid to take classes. Then you rotate through different operations within the facility.

You get exposed to all aspects of the trade. I did things as mundane as changing lighting fixtures and putting in electrical receptacles to hooking up and troubleshooting scientific machinery in the lab. Now each apprentice receives a book that requires you to perform certain tasks successfully. It has to be signed by your supervisor and journeyman.

What kinds of tasks are involved?

You have to hook up motors and other machinery. You troubleshoot and install equipment. You maintain robots and programmable controllers. It all involves computers now. We have programming units, essentially laptop computers, that you plug in and use as a diagnostic tool.

What did you do once you completed the apprenticeship?

I worked as a journeyman electrician and then as an electrical leader at Ford's Rouge plant, which manufactures cars as well as many of the components, including the glass and steel, that go into them.

What is your job now?

I have been an instructor for 13 years. I teach classes on programmable controllers, robot systems, computer programming and maintenance, spot welding technology, and stamping press automation.

How do you keep up with the technology changes?

Technology is galloping ahead. What you learn today will be obsolete in three to four years. That is why you need strong reading and computer skills.

What education do you suggest for young people entering the field?

To get into skilled trades at Ford, you must first be an employee with some years of service under your belt and apply for the apprenticeship. I suggest they take basic math, science, reading, and anything to do with computers at a local community college, because the tests to get in are very competitive.

Do you need to be mechanically inclined?

It helps to be mechanically inclined or interested in electric things. It helps if you are a tinkerer.

Is the job as open to women as men?

Yes. We have some very good women in the field.

What is the environment like?

People think of a factory as a turn-of-the-century forge mill with grease, oil, smoke, and heat everywhere. That's not what a modern manufacturing plant is like. Today's assembly plants are clean and relatively quiet.

What is the key to success in your field?

To be successful, you've got to be one who thrives on learning. You need good hand coordination to do some mechanical tasks. You have to get along with a wide range of people. Some are friendly; some are not. You have to be flexible on hours. When car sales are good, plants work overtime, and you may work 10 to 12 hours a day for long periods of time. The bonus is you receive overtime pay. The downside is that you miss time with the family.

What do you like most about working in this field?

The job I have currently is my favorite one, and I like constantly updating classes. I examine new equipment and design training classes around it. We build specialized simulators that mimic the machines, then we write the book and design the classes around it.

What is one of your proudest achievements?

When I worked as an electrician, I was basically running a small construction group. I took a lot of pride in putting in a new welding line and installing a big stamping press. It came in pieces, had to be installed and programmed. It took about three to five months. But I got great job satisfaction from just watching it run.

Will You Fit Into the World of Cars?

Before you enroll in a program of study or start to search for a job in one of the careers described in this book, it's smart to figure out whether that career is a good fit, given your background, skills, and personality. There are a number of ways to do this. They include:

❑ Talk to people who work in the field. Find out what they like and don't like about their jobs, what kinds of people their employers hire, and what their recommendations are about training

❑ Use a computer to help you identify career options. Some of the most widely used programs are *Discover*, by the American College Testing Service, *SIGI Plus*, developed by the Educational Testing Service, and *Peterson's Career & College Quest*. Some public libraries make this career software available to library users at low or no cost. The career counseling or guidance offices of your high school or local community college are other possibilities.

❑ Take a paper-and-pencil or online career assessment. There are different ones available, including the Strong Interest Inventory, the Self-Directed

Search, or the Career Assessment Inventory. You will be asked questions about your values, skills, aptitudes, and experiences. High schools, community colleges, and vocational/technical schools usually offer free assessments.

❏ Talk to a career counselor. You can find one by asking friends and colleagues if they know of any good ones. Or contact the career information office of the adult education division of a local college. Its staff members and workshop leaders often do one-on-one counseling. The job information services division of a major library sometimes offers low- or no-cost counseling by appointment. Or check the *Yellow Pages* under the heading "Vocational Guidance."

Before you spend time, energy, or money doing any of the above, take one or more of the following five quizzes (one for each career described in the book). The results can help you confirm whether you really are cut out to work in a particular career.

If a career in CAD (computer-aided design) interests you, take this quiz:

Read each statement, then choose the number 0, 5, or 10. The rating scale below explains what each number means.

0=Disagree
5=Agree somewhat
10=Strongly agree

__ I understand how a car operates.

__ I enjoy working on computers and understand how to use them.

__ I have good powers of concentration.

__ I think I am capable of working alone for long periods of time in front of a computer screen.

__ I am good at asking questions and following directions.

__ I like to identify problems and find a solution for them.

__ I am meticulous in terms of neatness, accuracy, and attention to detail.

__ I have strong math skills, especially algebra, geometry, and trigonometry.

__ I've worked with factory machines to make parts in shop class.

__ I have a strong background in science, including physics and chemistry.

Now add up your score. ____Total points

If your total points were less than 50, you probably do not have sufficient interest or inclination to learn what's required to go into computer-aided design. If your total points were between 50 and 75, you may have what it takes to get into computer-aided design, but be sure to do more investigation by following the suggestions at the beginning of this section. If your total points were above 75, it's highly likely that you are a good candidate to work in the field of computer-aided design.

If vehicle sales interests you, take this quiz:

Read each statement, then choose the number 0, 5, or 10. The rating scale below explains what each number means.

> 0=Disagree
> 5=Agree somewhat
> 10=Strongly agree

__ I love talking about cars and learning about the newest automotive technology.

__ I am a disciplined and highly motivated person.

__ I have a friendly, outgoing personality.

__ I'm not afraid of approaching people I don't know by phone or in person.

__ I have sales experience.

__ I like explaining the details of a product to a customer.

__ I have a persuasive manner.

__ I don't take rejection personally.

__ I'm willing to work long hours.

__ I'm good at negotiating and making compromises.

Now add up your score. ____Total points

If your total points were less than 50, you probably do not have what it takes to become a successful car salesperson. If your total points were between 50 and 75, you may have what it takes to get into automobile sales, but be sure to do more investigation by following the suggestions at the beginning of this section. If your total points were above 75, it's highly likely that you are a good candidate to work in the field of automobile sales.

If a career as an auto mechanic interests you, take this quiz:

Read each statement, then choose the number 0, 5, or 10. The rating scale below explains what each number means.

0=Disagree
5=Agree somewhat
10=Strongly agree

__ I'm good at taking things apart and putting them back together.

__ I like working with my hands and am good at it.

__ I don't mind getting dirty.

__ I know how to work with tools.

__ I understand how a car operates.

__ I have no fear of using computers.

__ I have good reading skills.

__ I like figuring out where a problem exists and how to solve it.

__ I like to stick with a problem or task until it is completed.

__ I am good at asking questions.

Now add up your score. ____Total points

If your total points were less than 50, you probably do not have sufficient interest or inclination to learn what's required to become an auto mechanic. If your total points were between 50 and 75, you may have what it takes to get into auto mechanics, but be sure to do more investigation by following the suggestions at the beginning of this section. If your total points were above 75, it's highly likely that you are a good candidate to work in the field of auto mechanics.

If a career as an auto claims representative interests you, take this quiz:

Read each statement, then choose the number 0, 5, or 10. The rating scale below explains what each number means.

> 0=Disagree
> 5=Agree somewhat
> 10=Strongly agree

__ I am a good listener.

__ I have some understanding of or am interested in learning about auto mechanics and auto body repair.

__ I have a basic understanding of how insurance works.

__ I am open minded and able to make an objective judgment after obtaining the facts about a situation.

__ I'm not shy about asking people personal questions.

__ I am able to negotiate with people to come up with a solution that's acceptable to all.

__ I know the basics of using a computer.

__ I remain calm when others around me are upset.

__ I'm good at taking notes.

__ I am observant; I notice the tiniest of details.

Now add up your score. ____Total points

If your total points were less than 50, you probably do not have sufficient interest of inclination to learn what's required to become an auto insurance claims representative. If your total points were between 50 and 75, you may have what it takes to get into auto insurance claims, but be sure to do more investigation by following the suggestions at the beginning of this section. If your total points were above 75, it's highly likely that you are a good candidate to work in the field of automobile insurance claims.

If a career as an auto electronics specialist interests you, take this quiz:

Read each statement, then choose the number 0, 5, or 10. The rating scale below explains what each number means.

> 0=Disagree
> 5=Agree somewhat
> 10=Strongly agree

__ I enjoy using computers.

__ I enjoy working with electronic equipment.

__ I know how to work with tools.

__ I would enjoy taking math, science, and computer courses.

__ I have patience to keep working until I find a solution to a problem.

__ I like working with my hands and am good at it.

__ I am meticulous in my attention to detail.

__ I can get along well with a variety of people and work with them.

__ I don't mind getting dirty.

__ I like the idea of working in a factory environment

Now add up your score. ____Total points

If your total points were less than 50, you probably do not have what it takes to become an electronics specialist. If your total points were between 50 and 75, you may have what it takes to get into auto electronics, but be sure to do more investigation by following the suggestions at the beginning of this section. If your total points were above 75, it's highly likely that you can be a success as an auto electronics specialist.

About the Author

Michelle Krebs is a Detroit-based freelance writer specializing in automotive coverage for newspapers, magazines, and book publishers.

She is a regular contributor and columnist for *The New York Times*, *Motor Trend* magazine, and the weekly industry trade journal, *Automotive News*. Her syndicated automotive column, *Down the Road*, runs in more than thirty newspapers in North America.

She started covering the auto industry as business editor of the *Oakland Press*, a daily newspaper in Pontiac, Michigan, a suburb of Detroit. She then became a staff writer and financial editor for *Automotive News*.